Doodling & Coloring Designs:

Mandalas

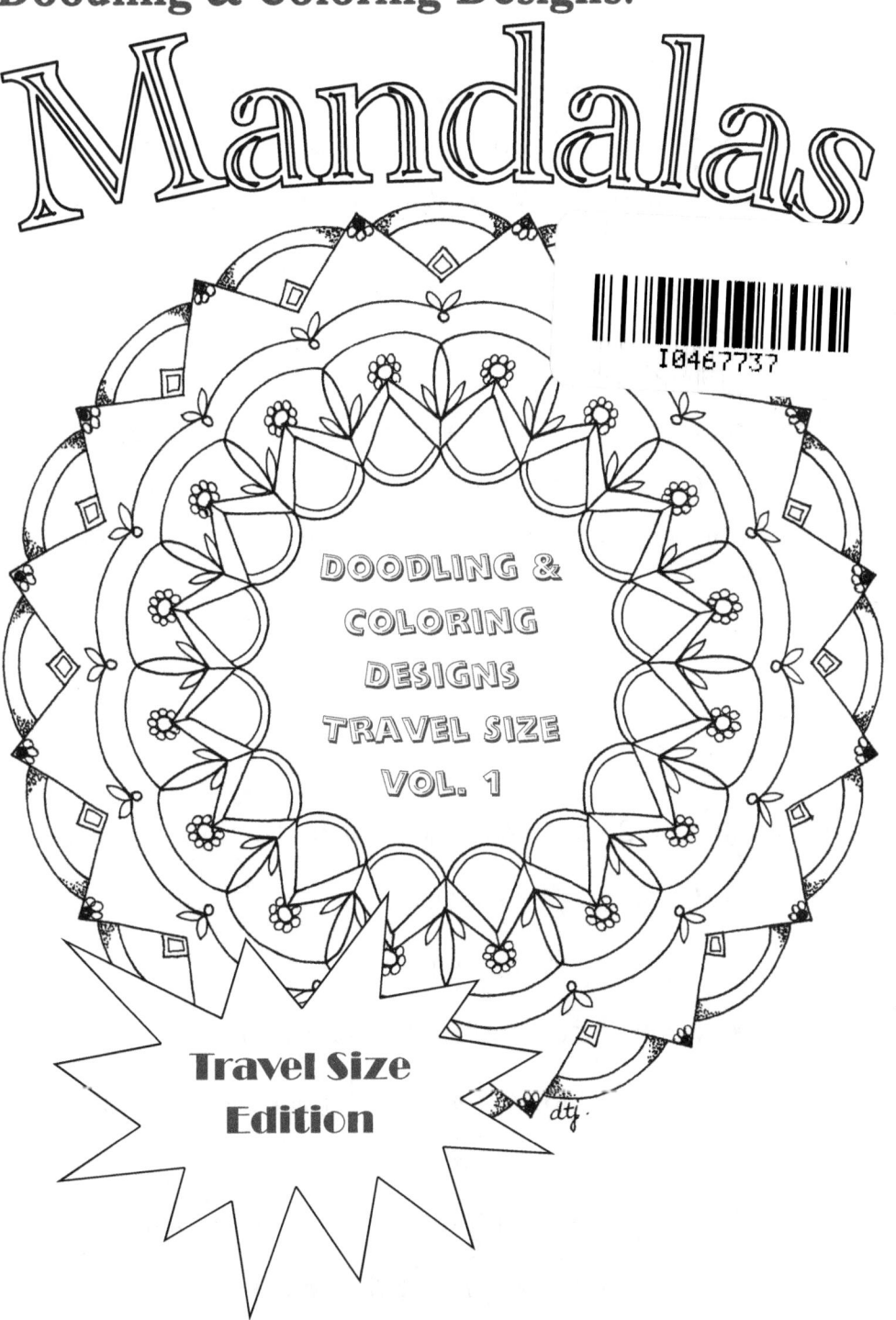

DOODLING &
COLORING
DESIGNS
TRAVEL SIZE
VOL. 1

Travel Size
Edition

Dedication

This coloring book is dedicated to:

My Facebook Group – "Doodling & Coloring Designs".... They are a wonderfully creative bunch of people who share in this passion and art form.

Authors note: I highly recommend that you place a sheet of card stock behind the page that you are coloring to prevent bleed through of markers or gel pens on to the next coloring page.

Printed by CreateSpace, An Amazon.com Company

Copyright © 2015 Darla Sue Tjelmeland

Contact the author if there are any questions.

ISBN-13: 978-1522820994

ISBN-10: 152282099X

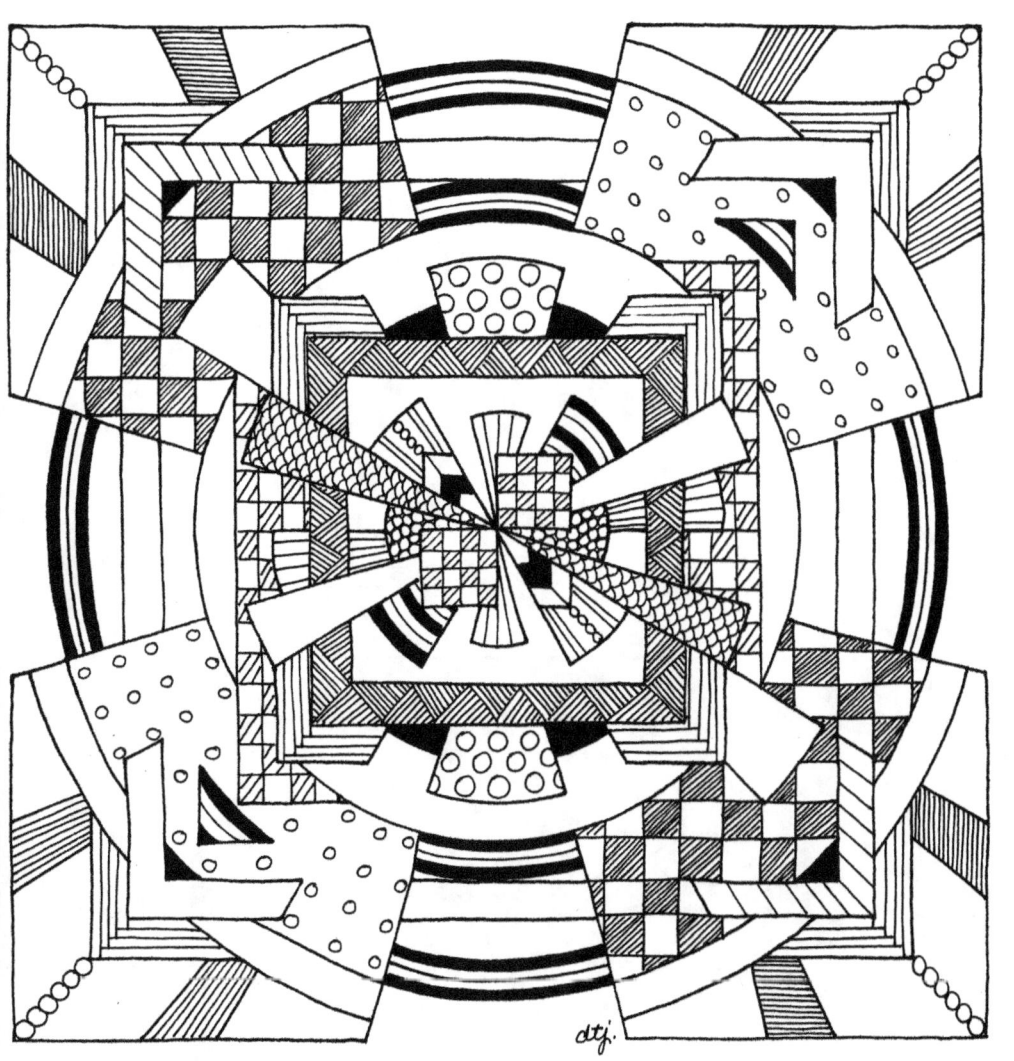

3

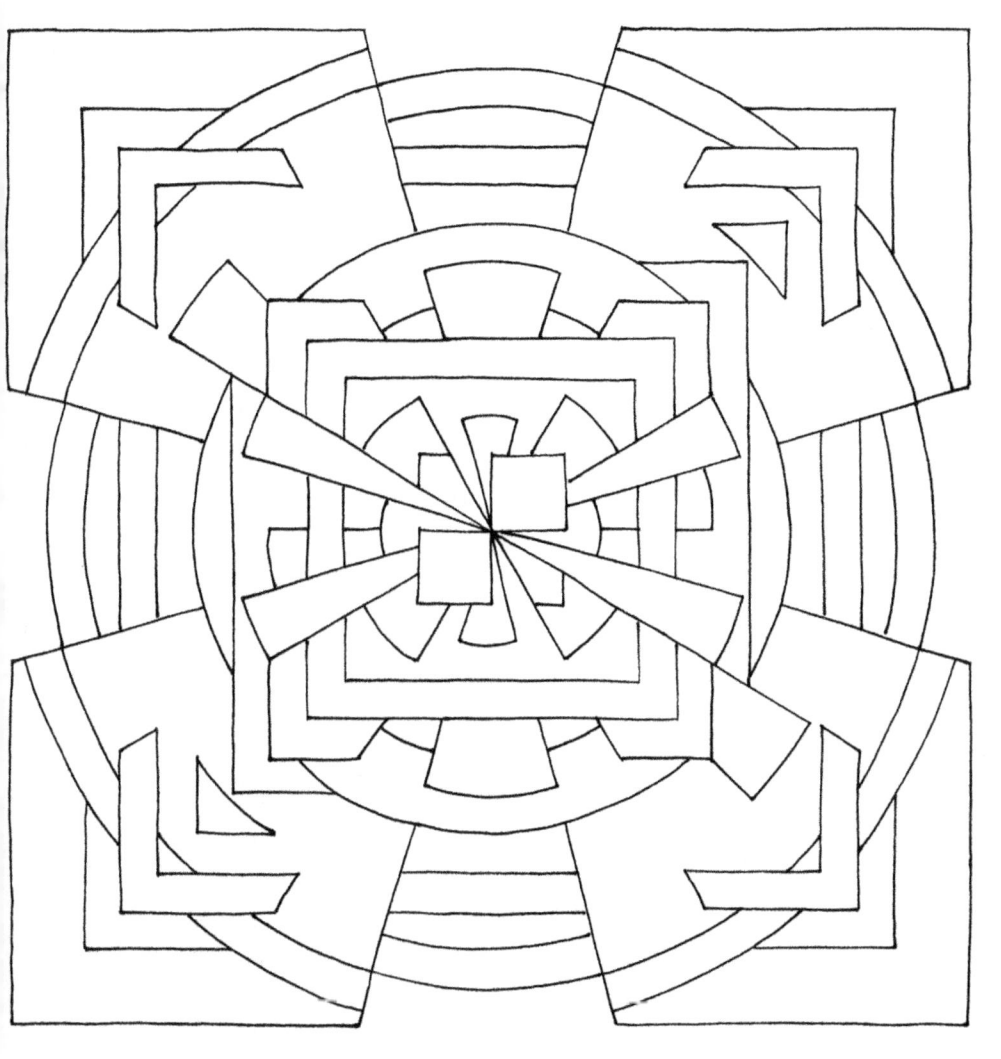

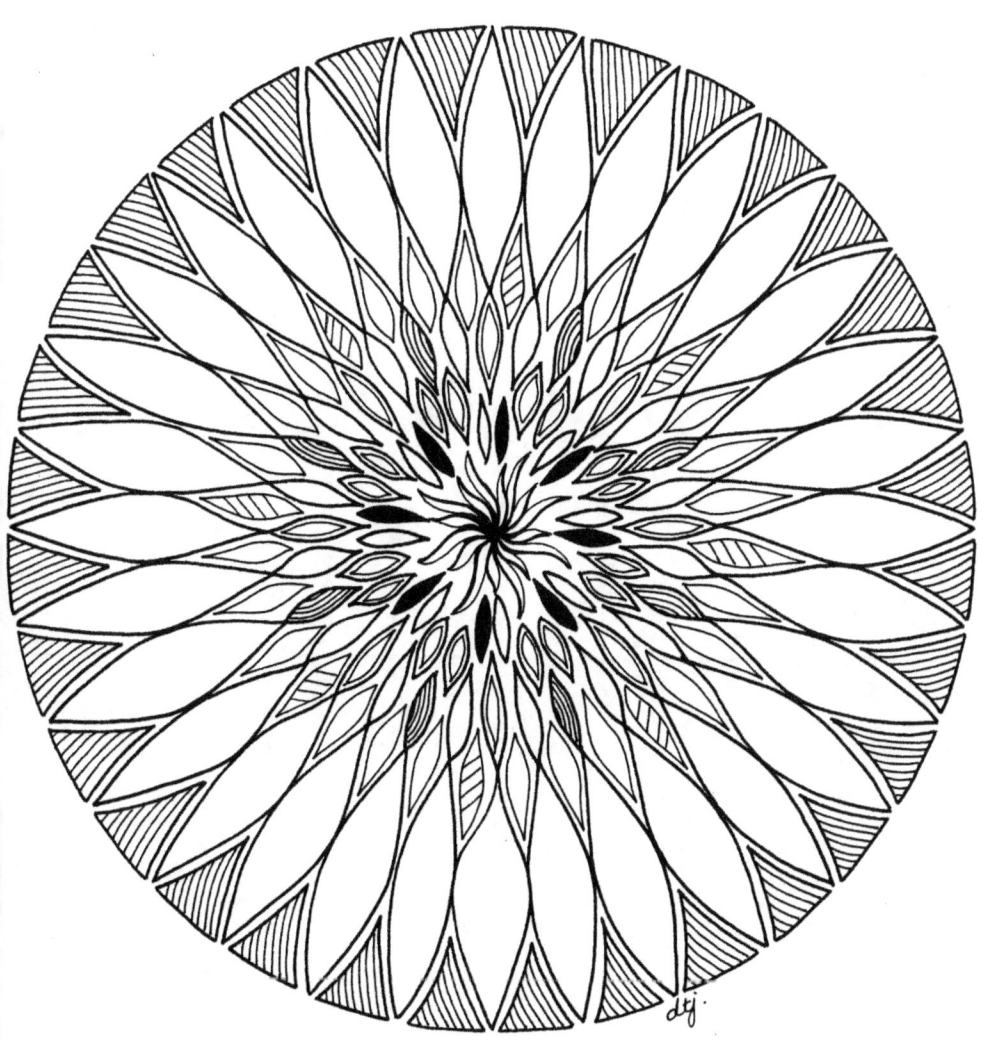

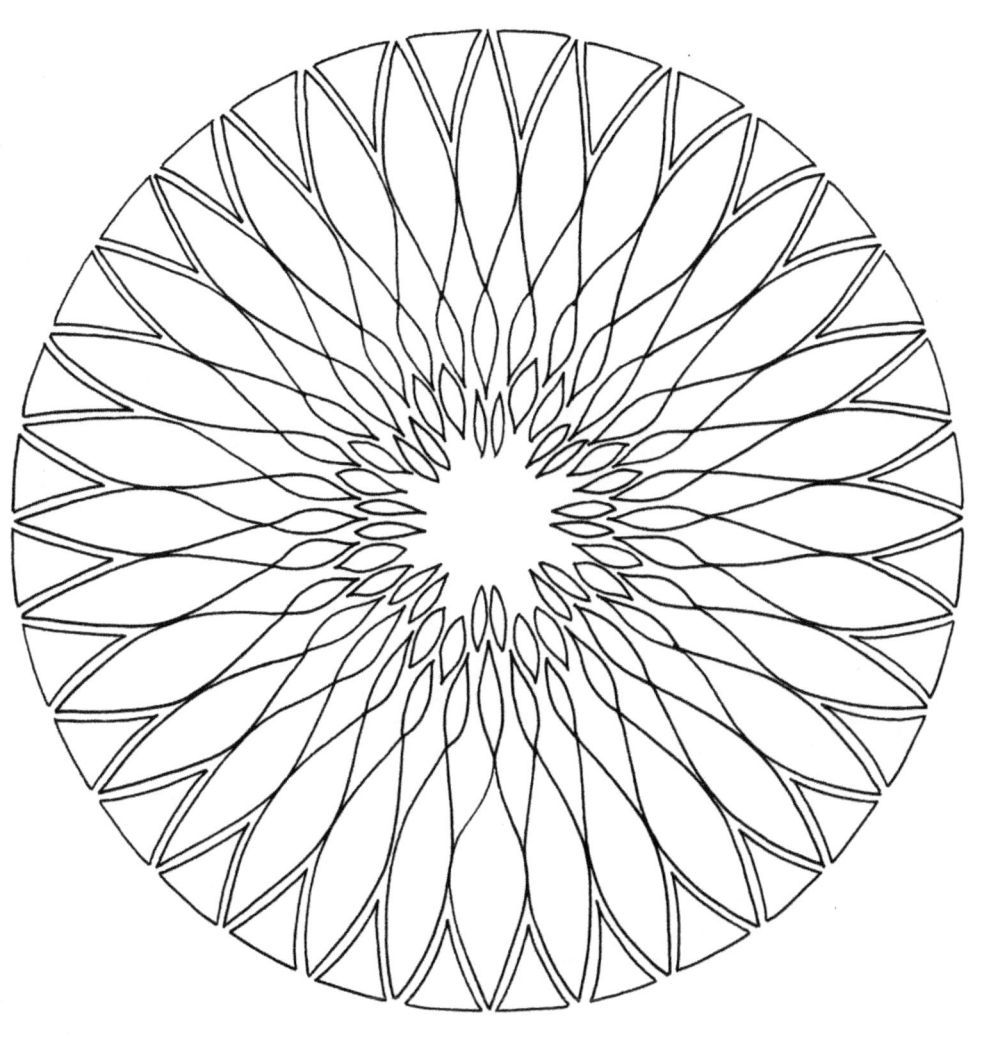

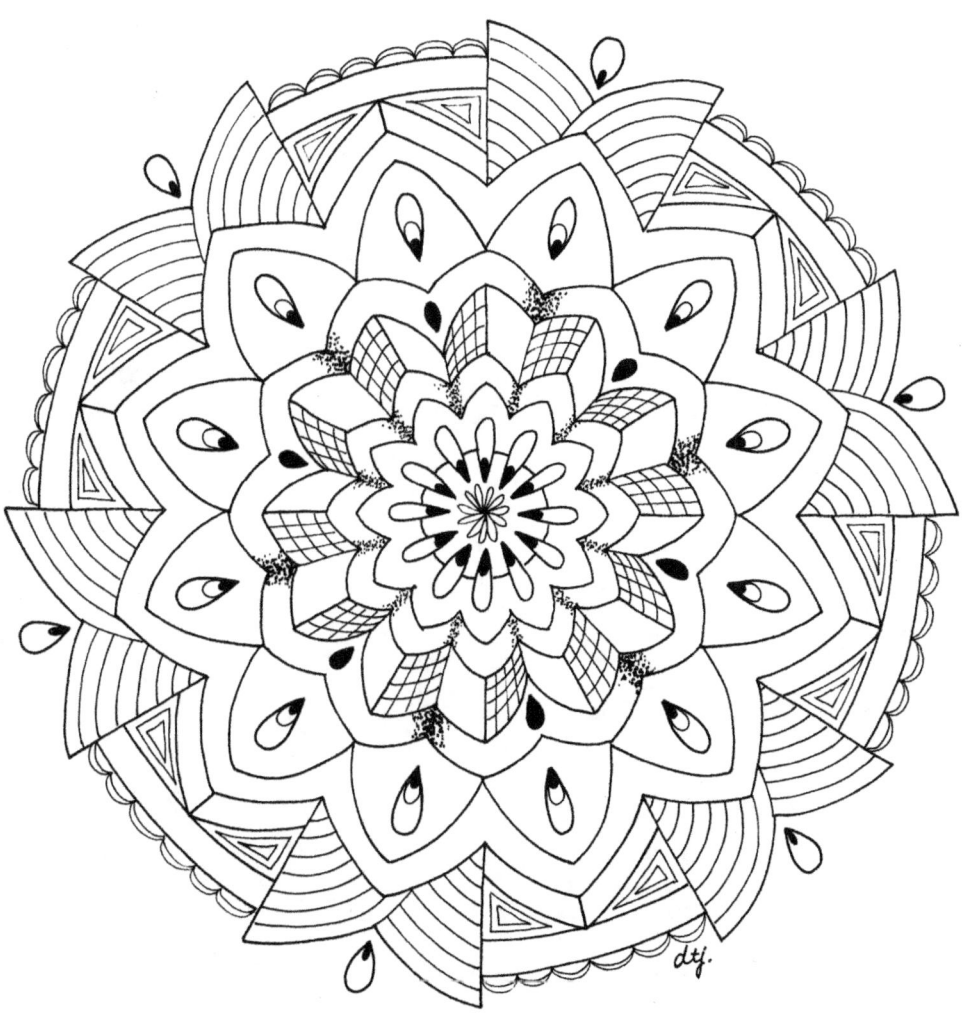

11

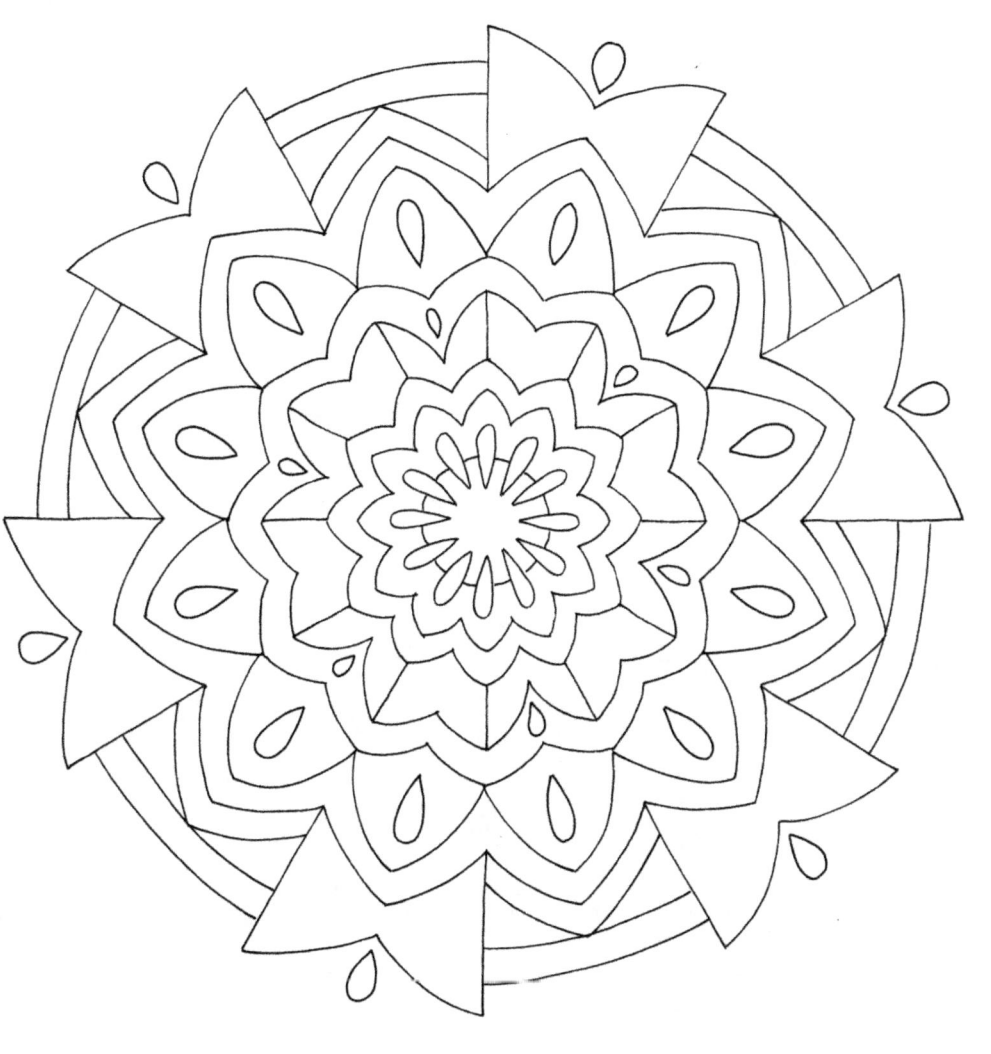

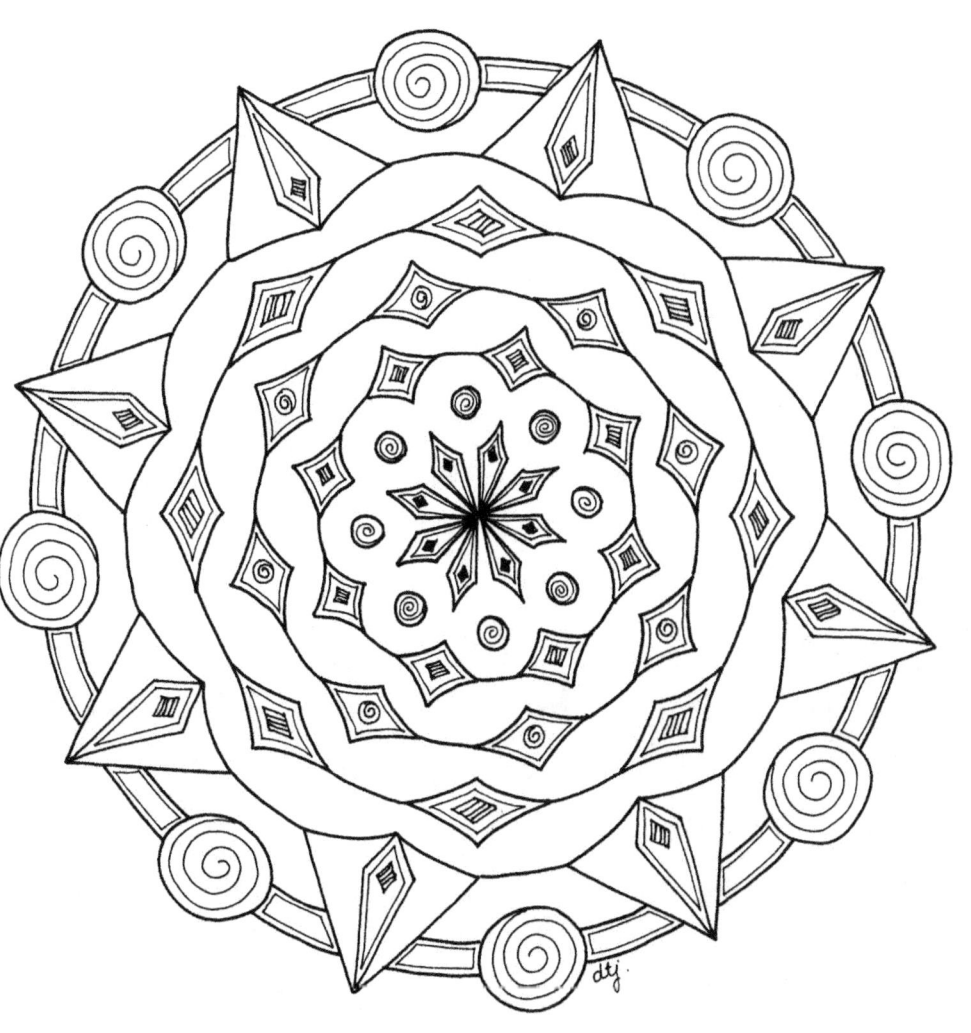

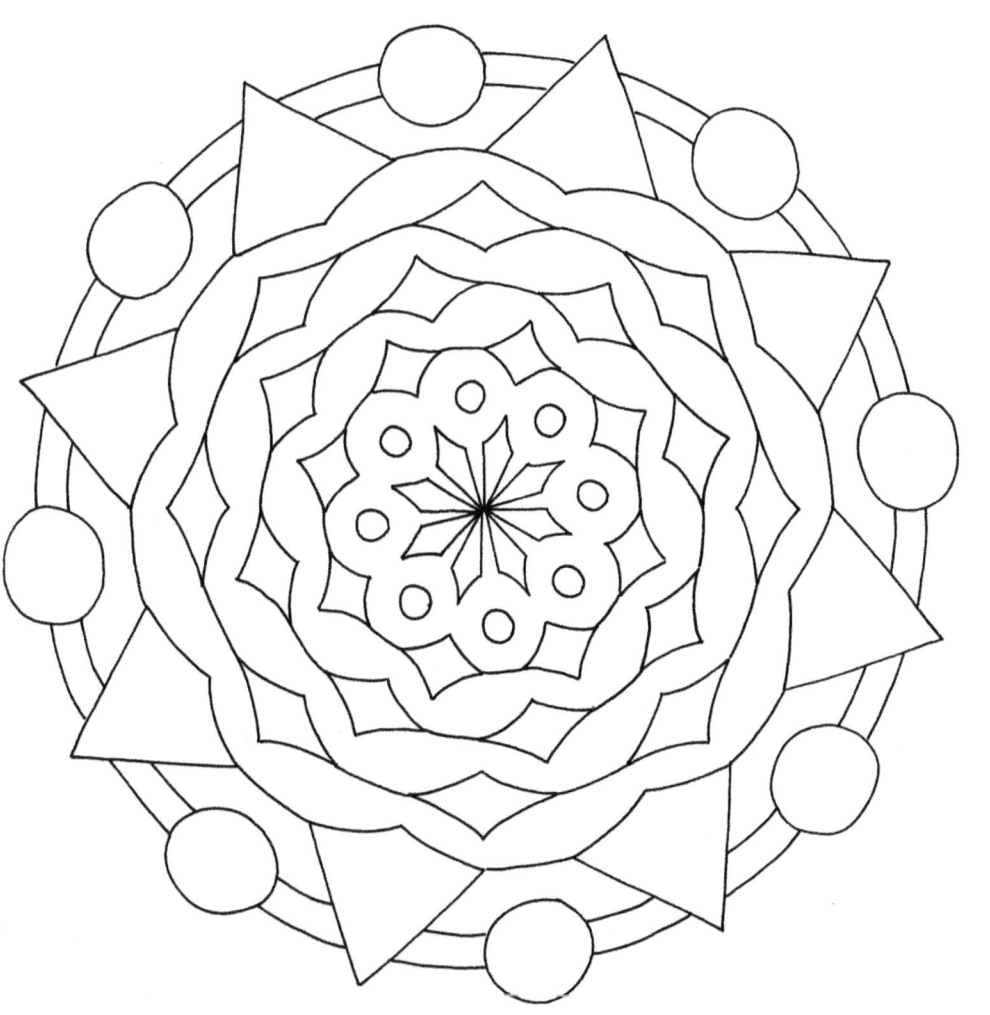

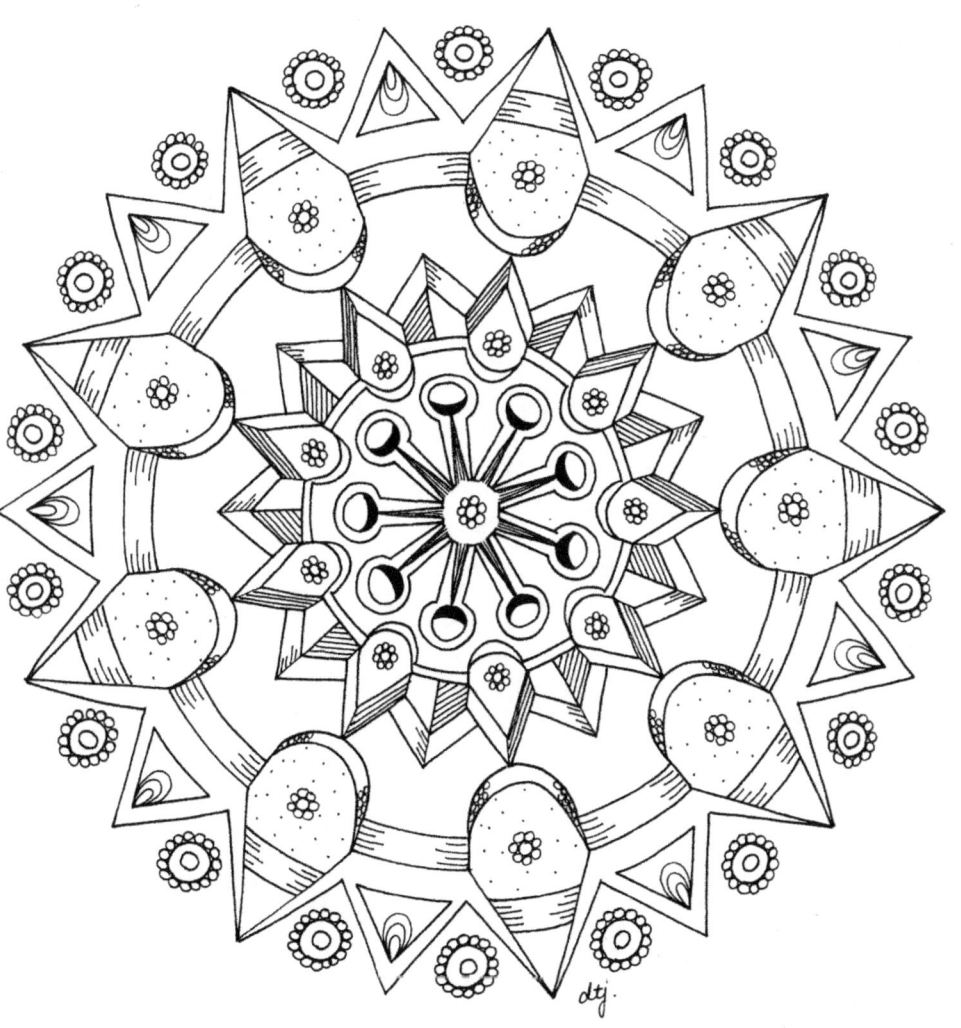

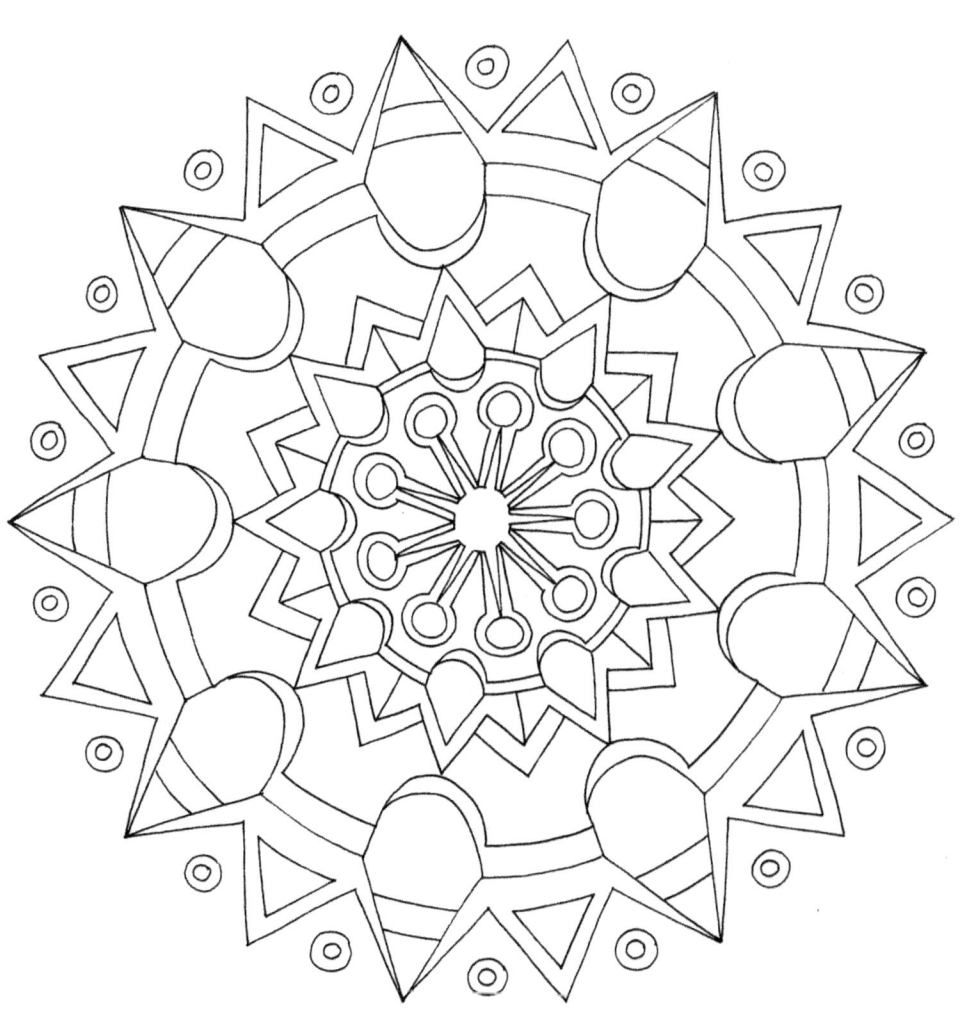

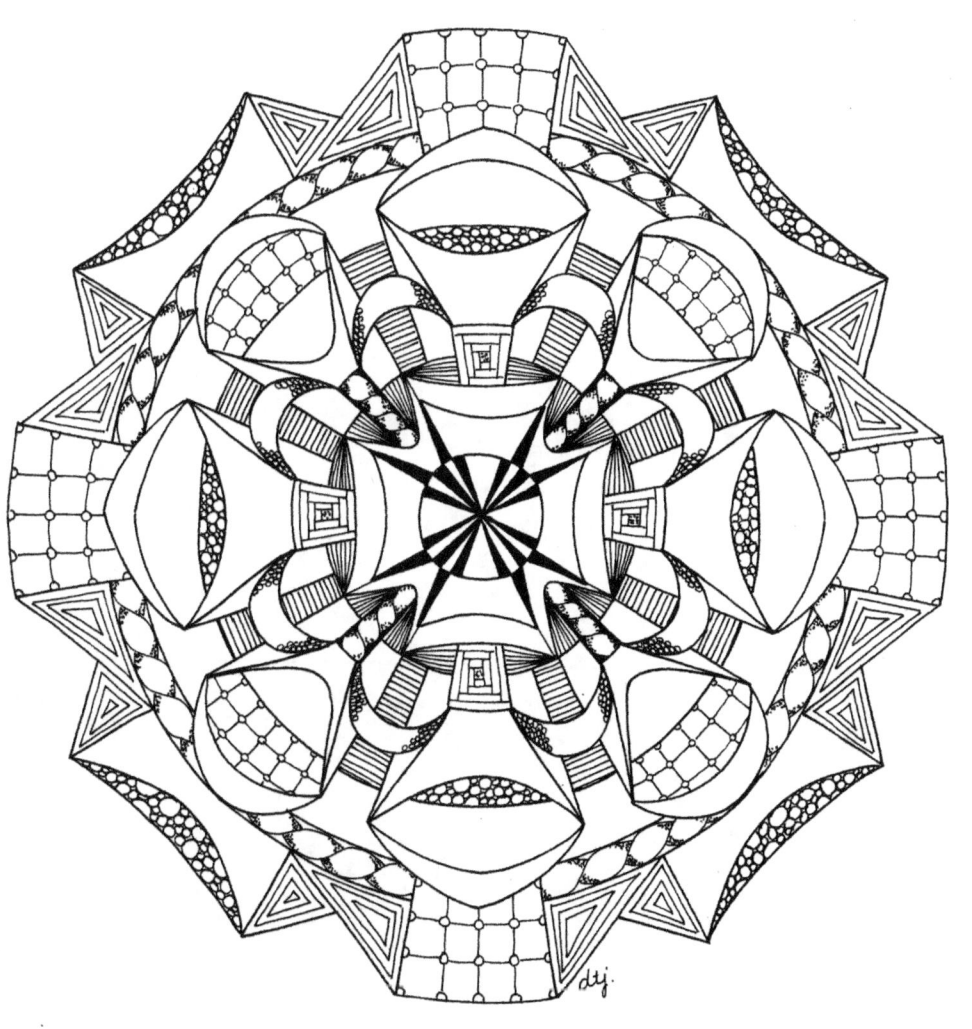

23

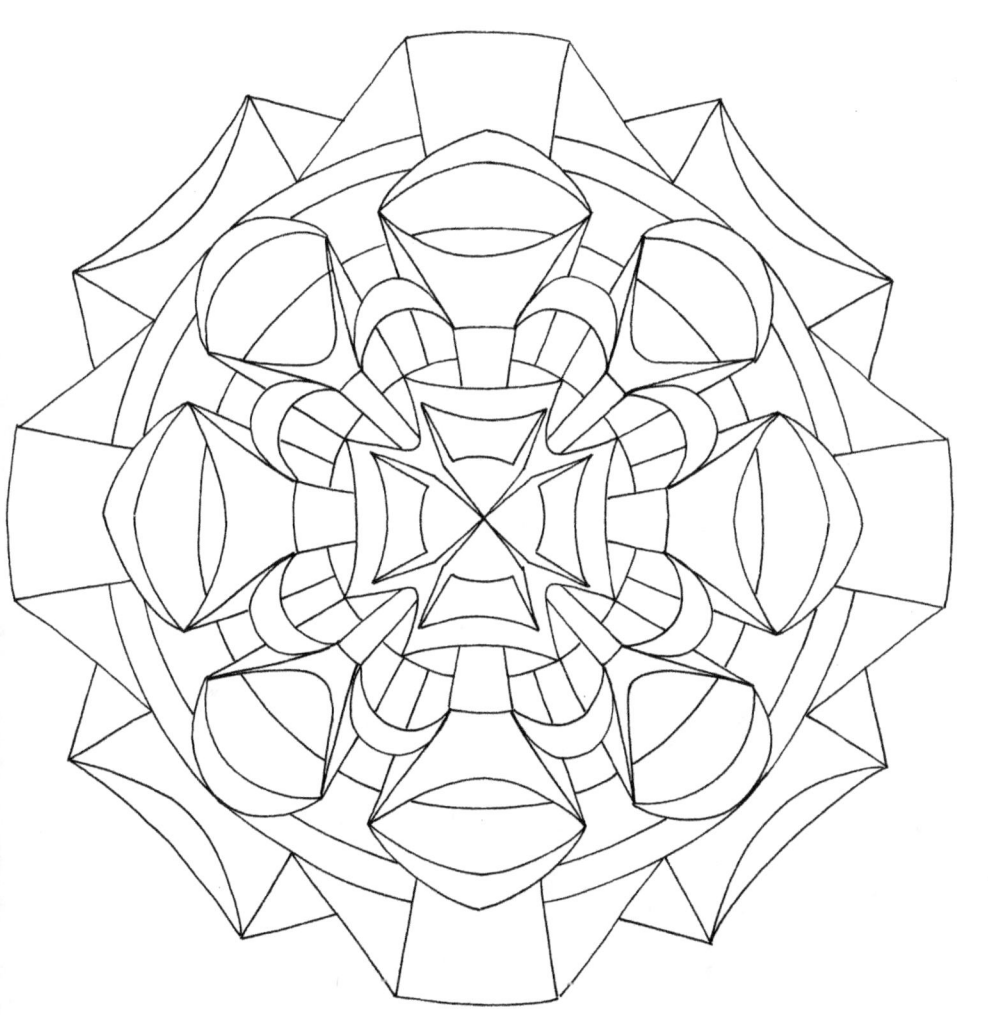

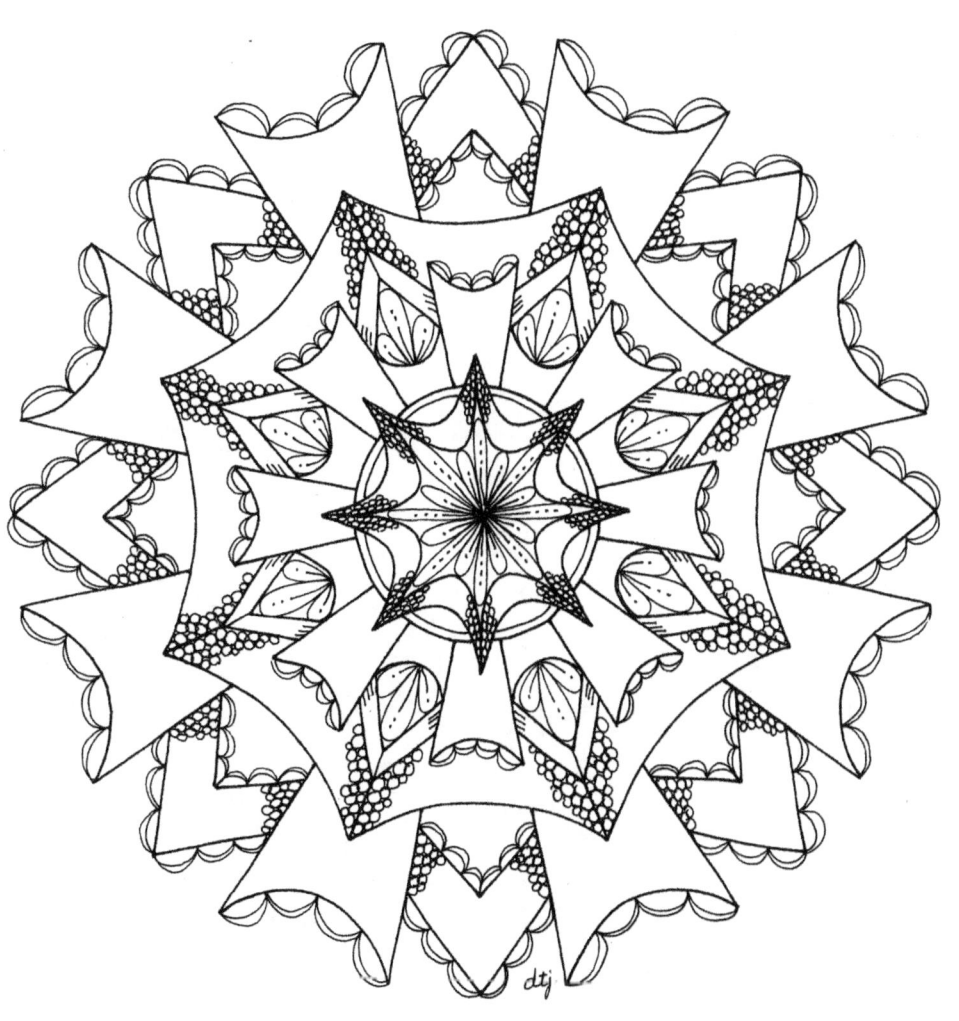

27

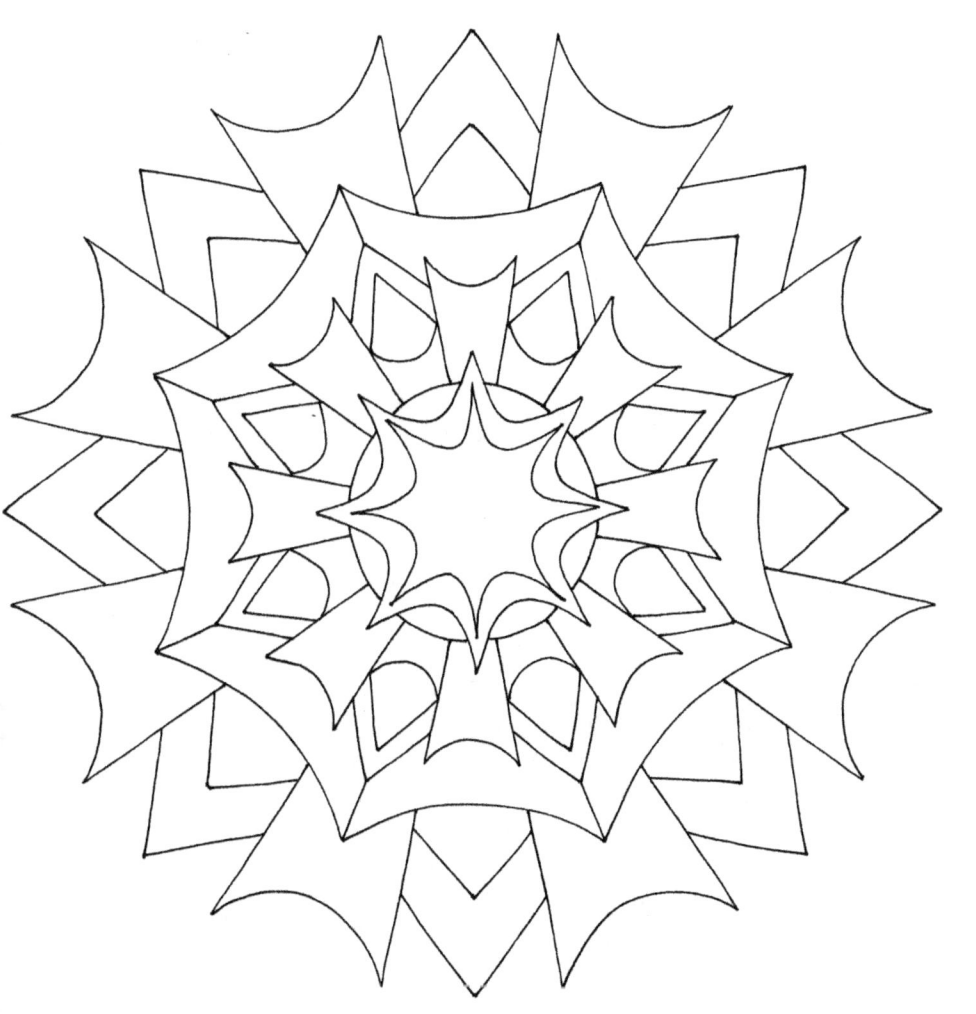

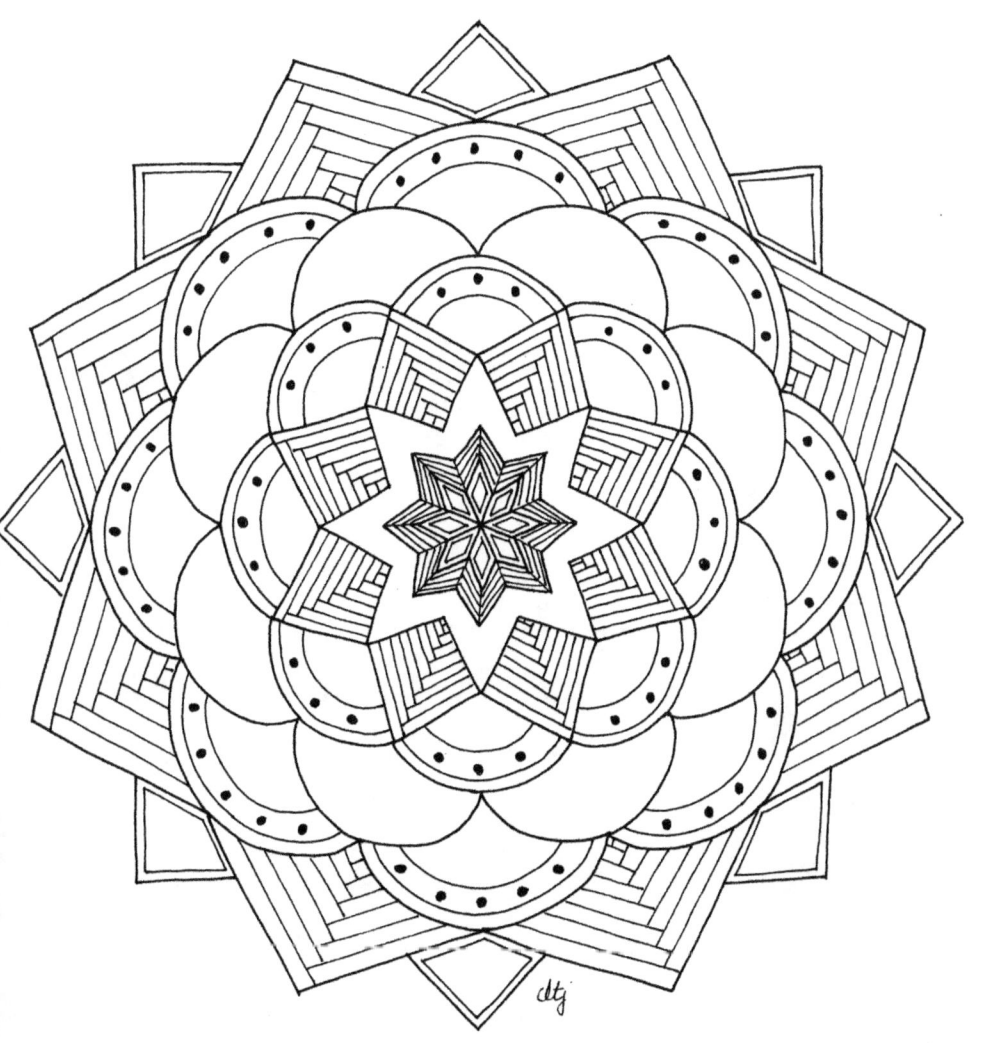

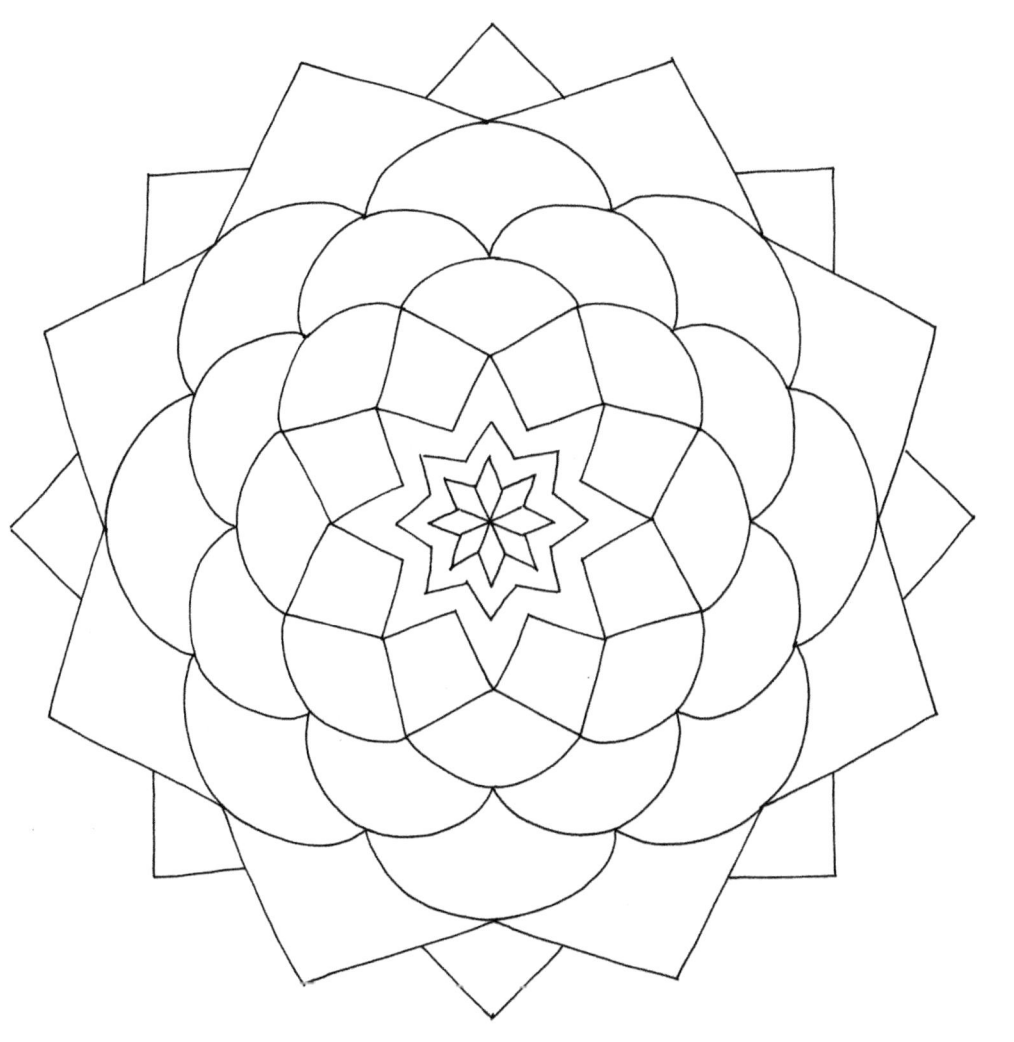

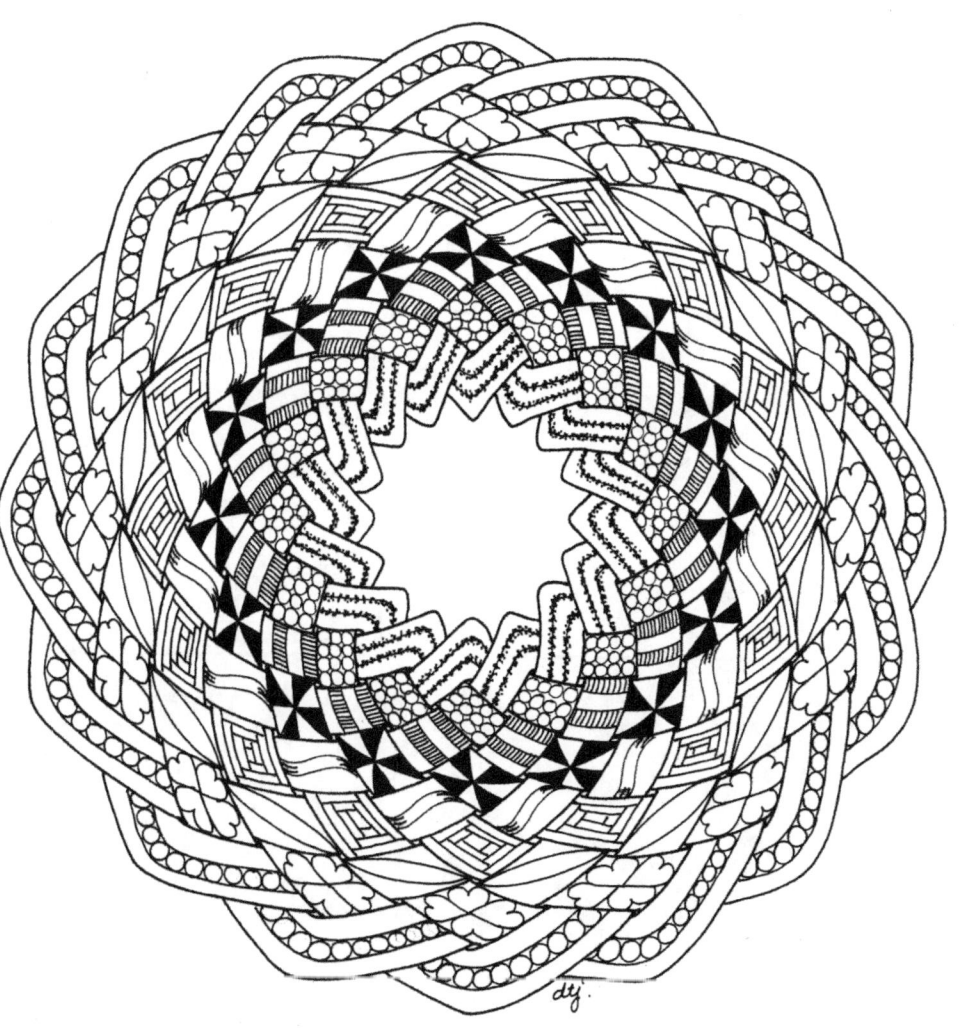

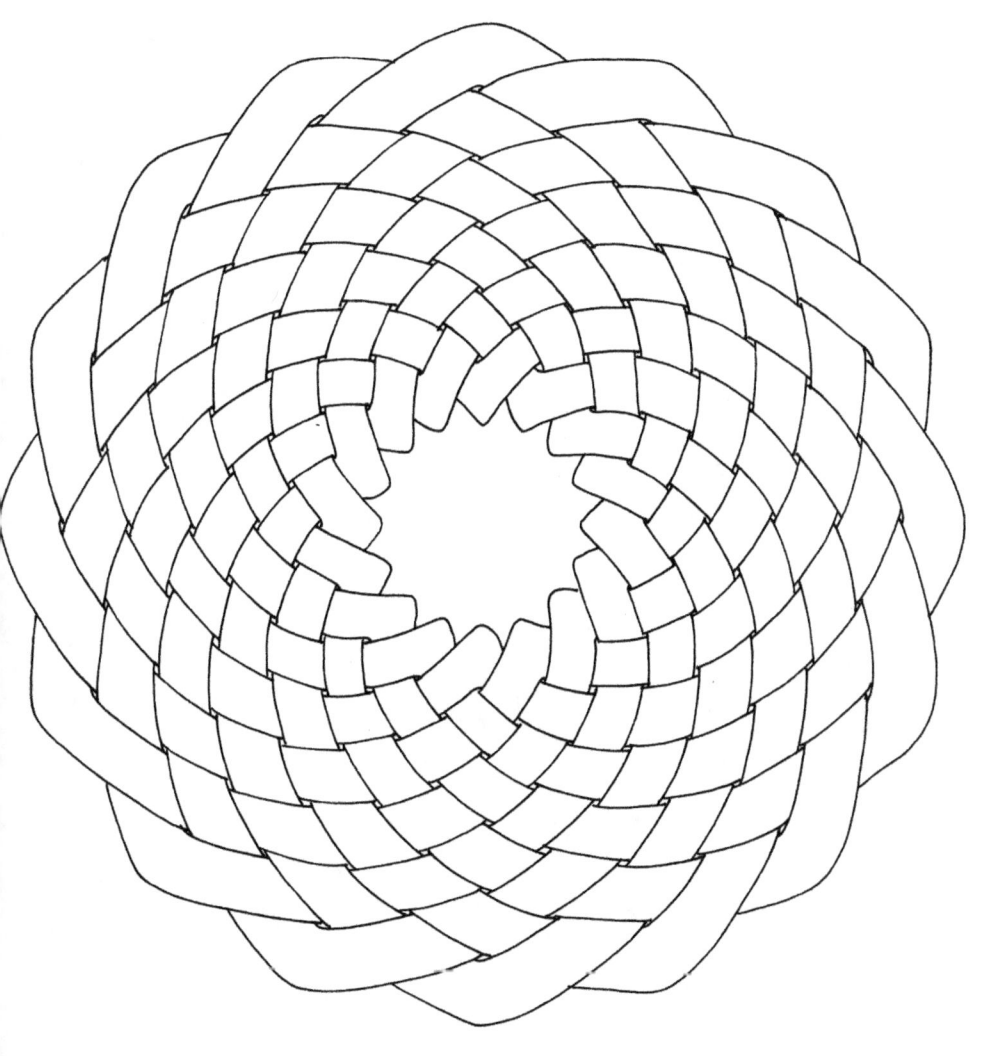

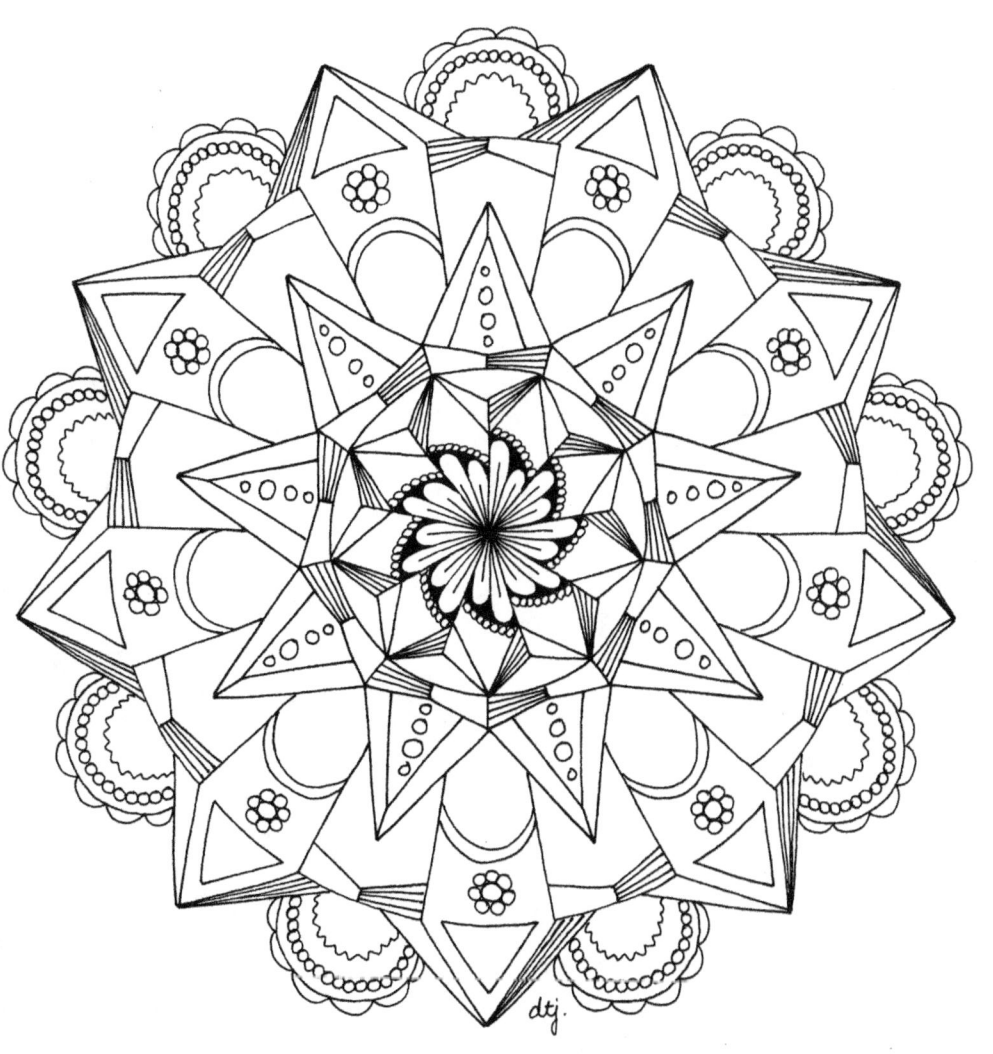

39

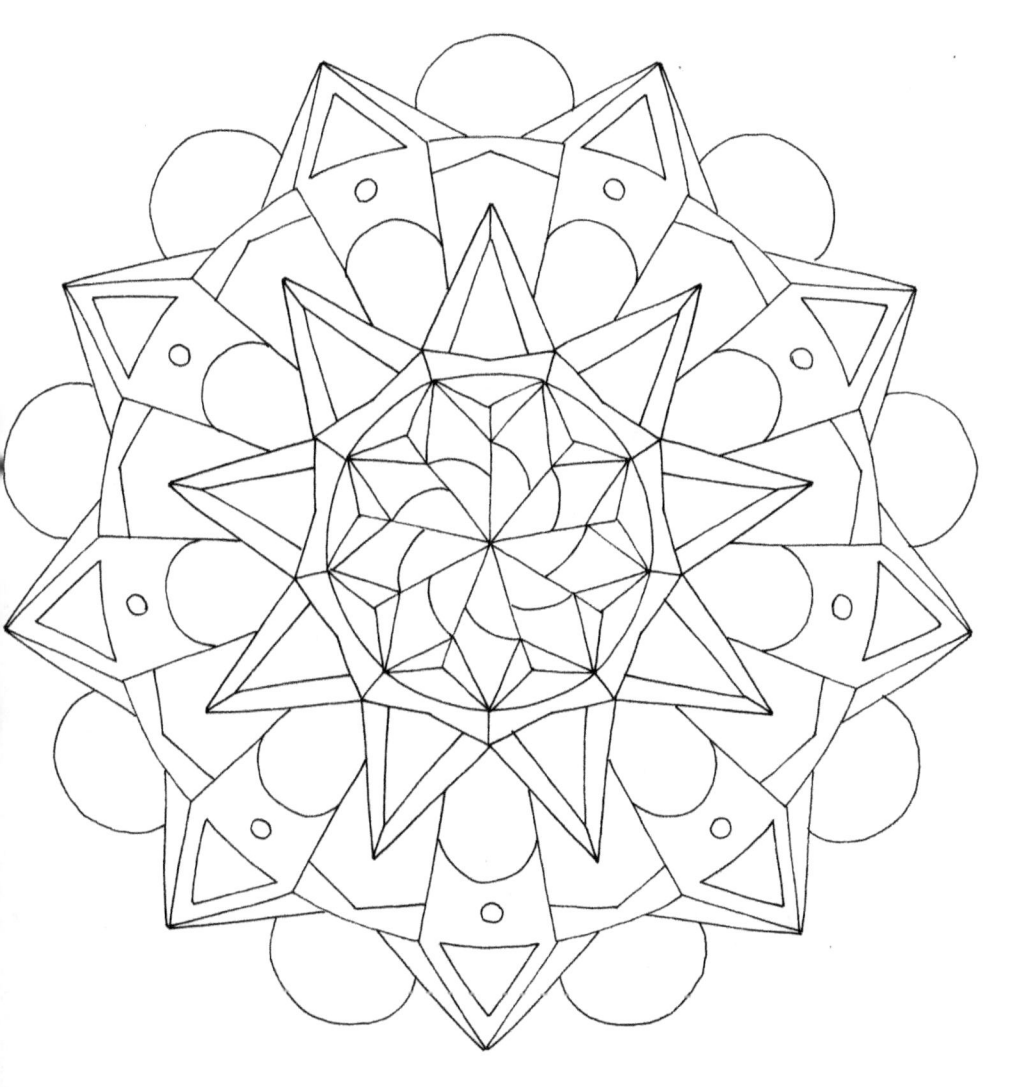

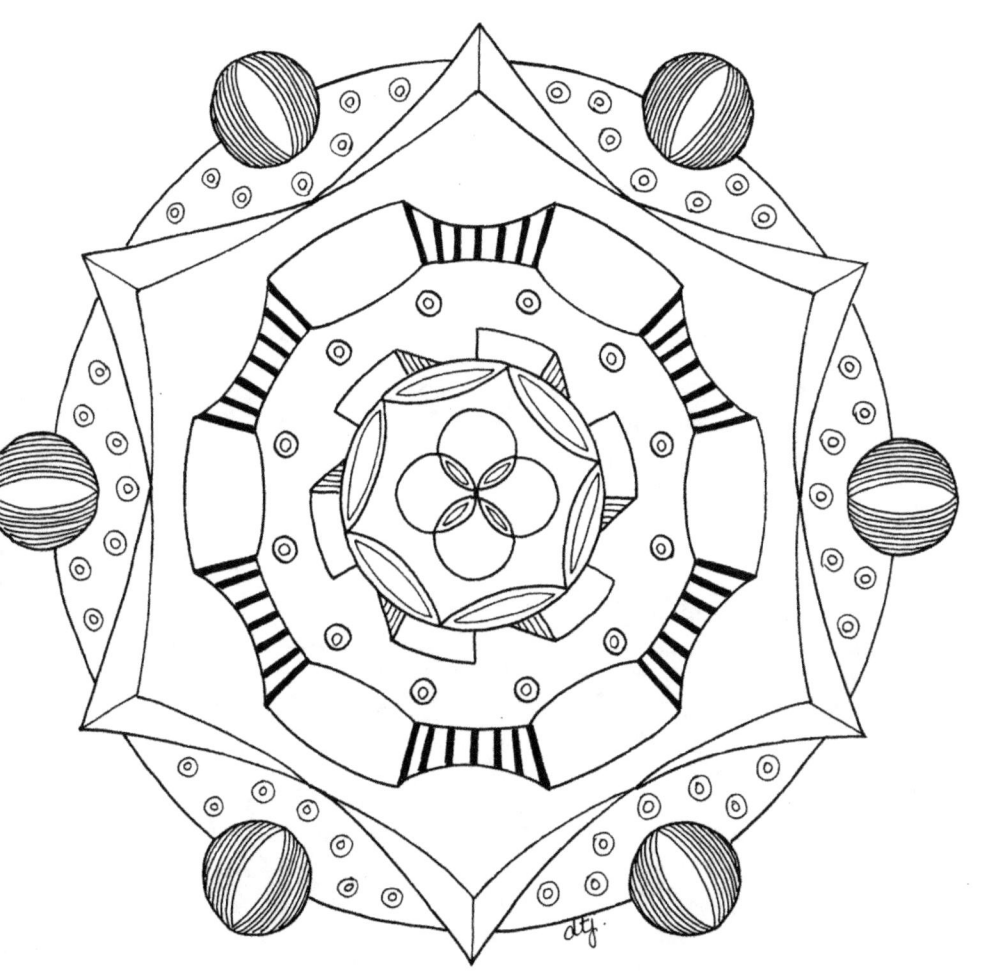

43

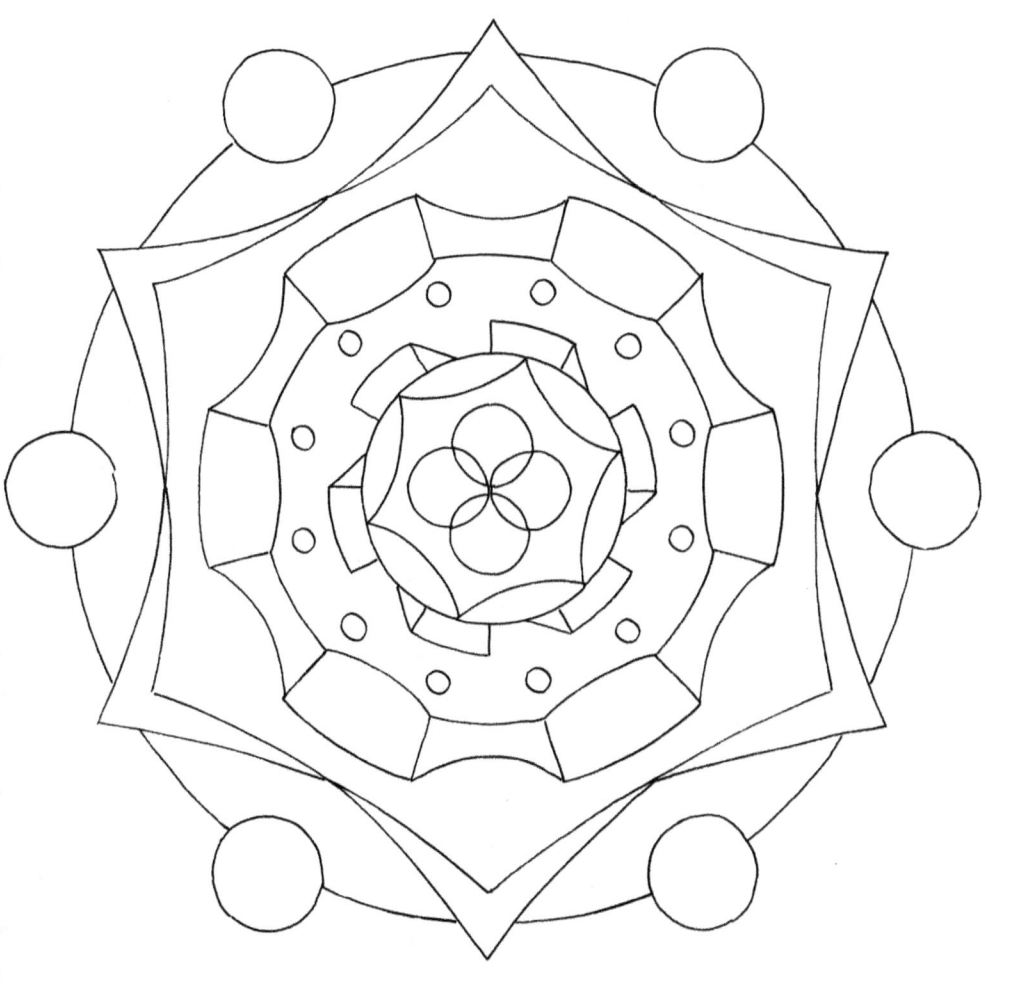

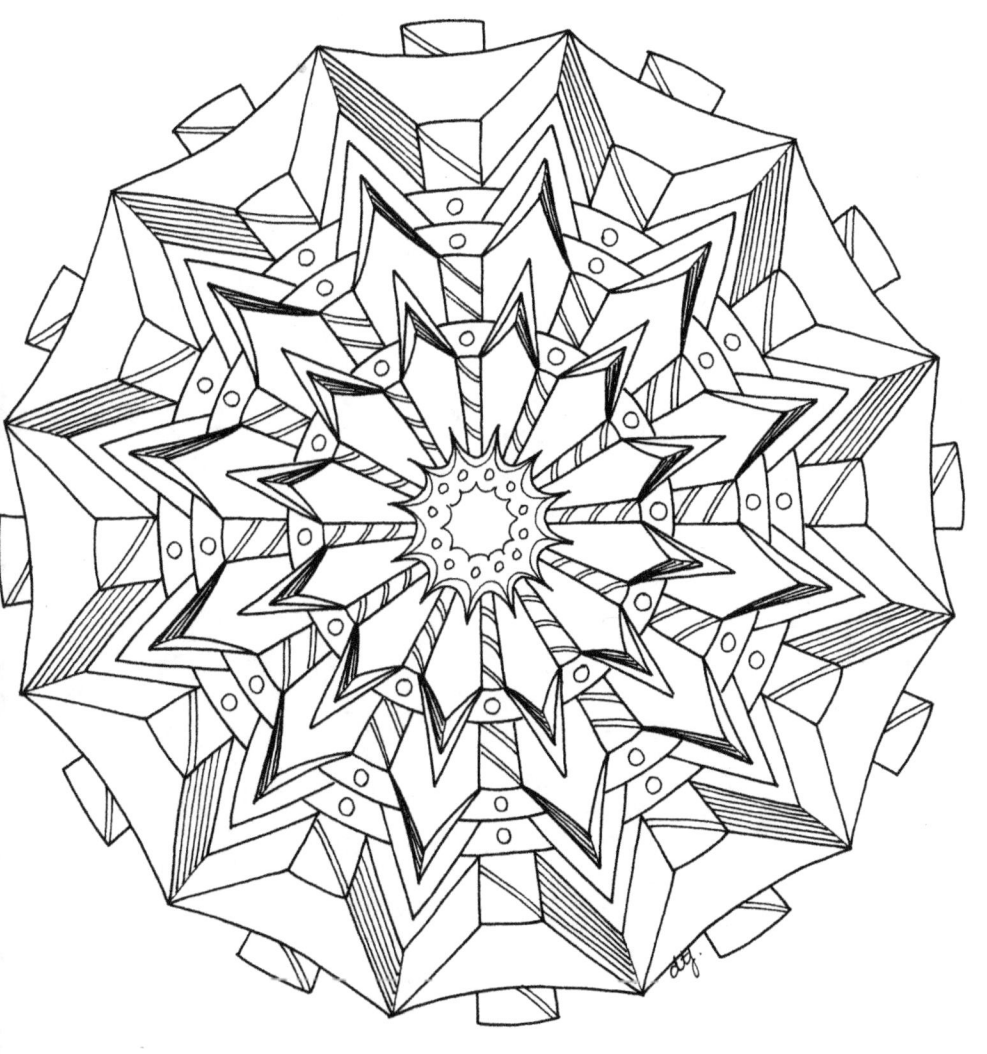

47

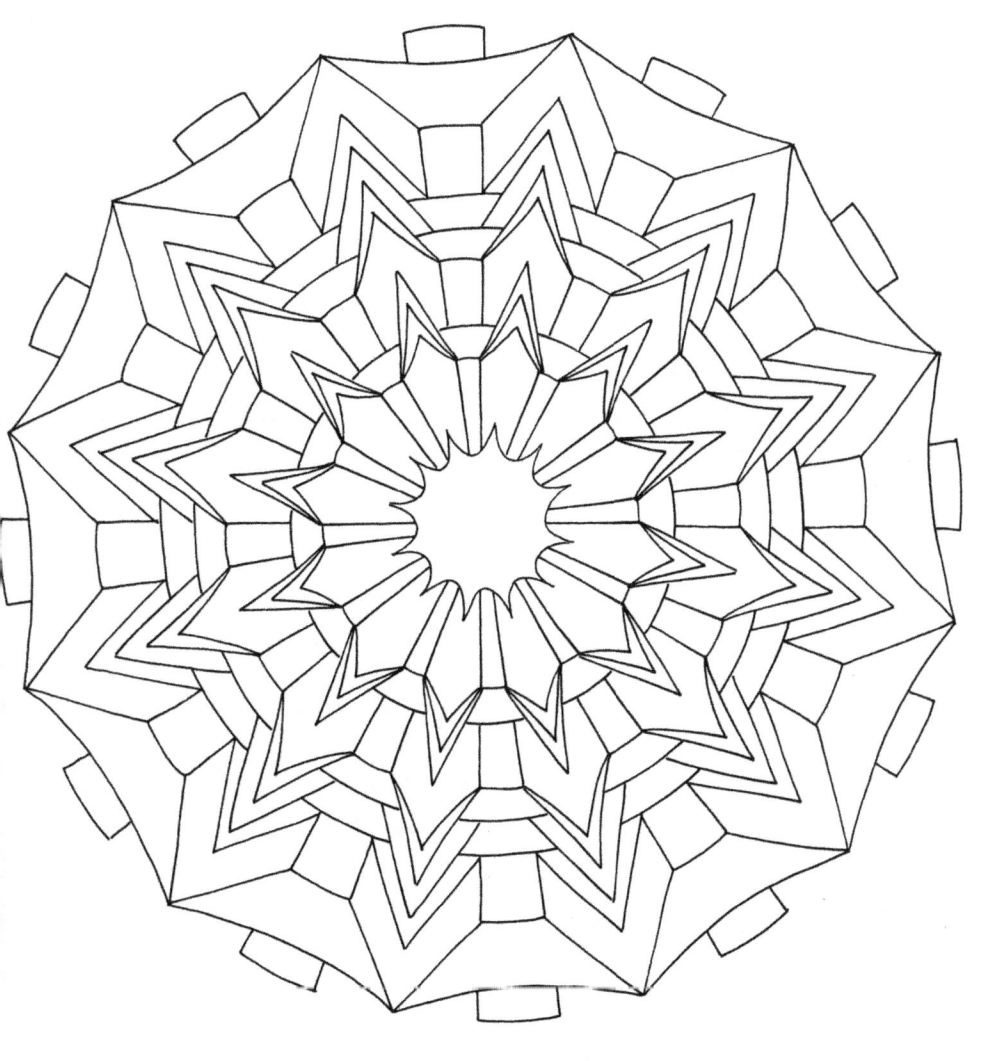

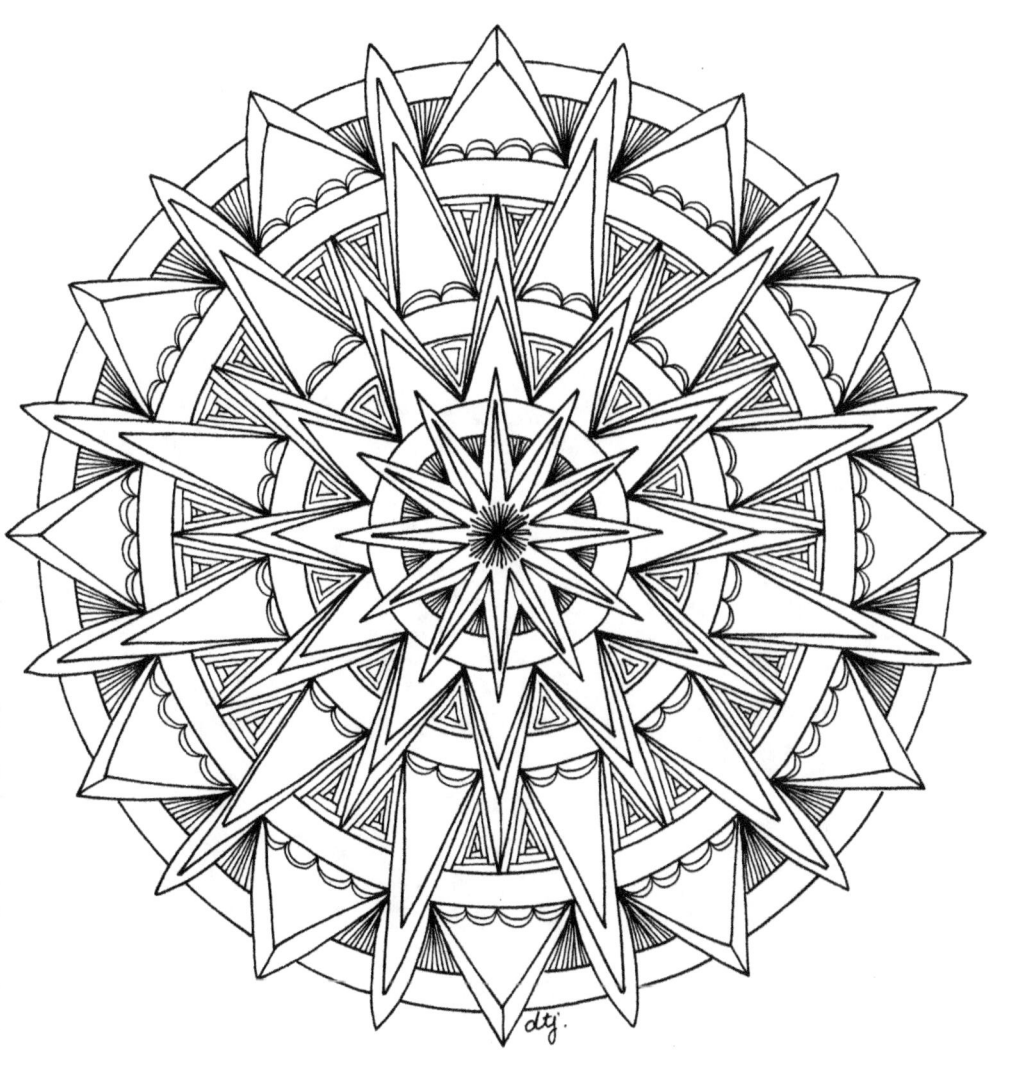

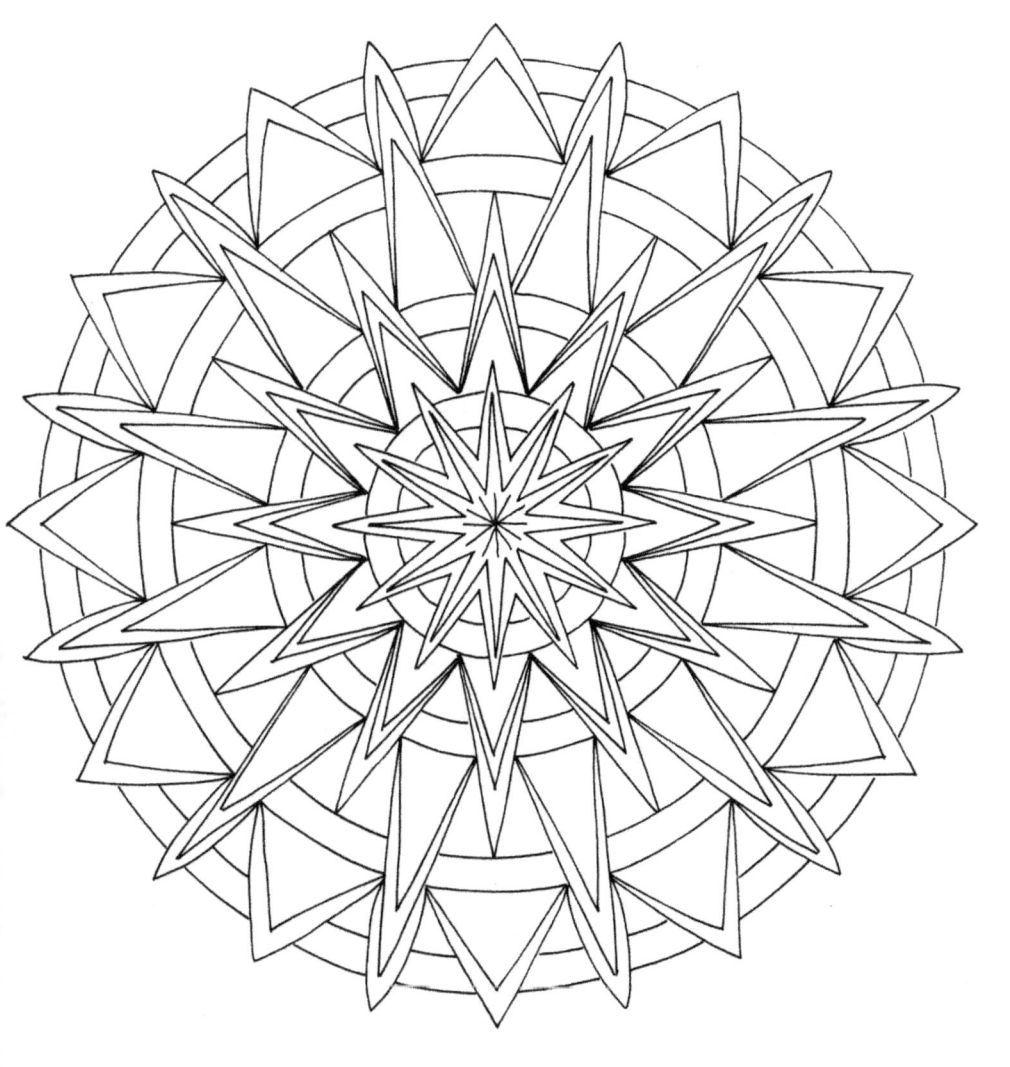

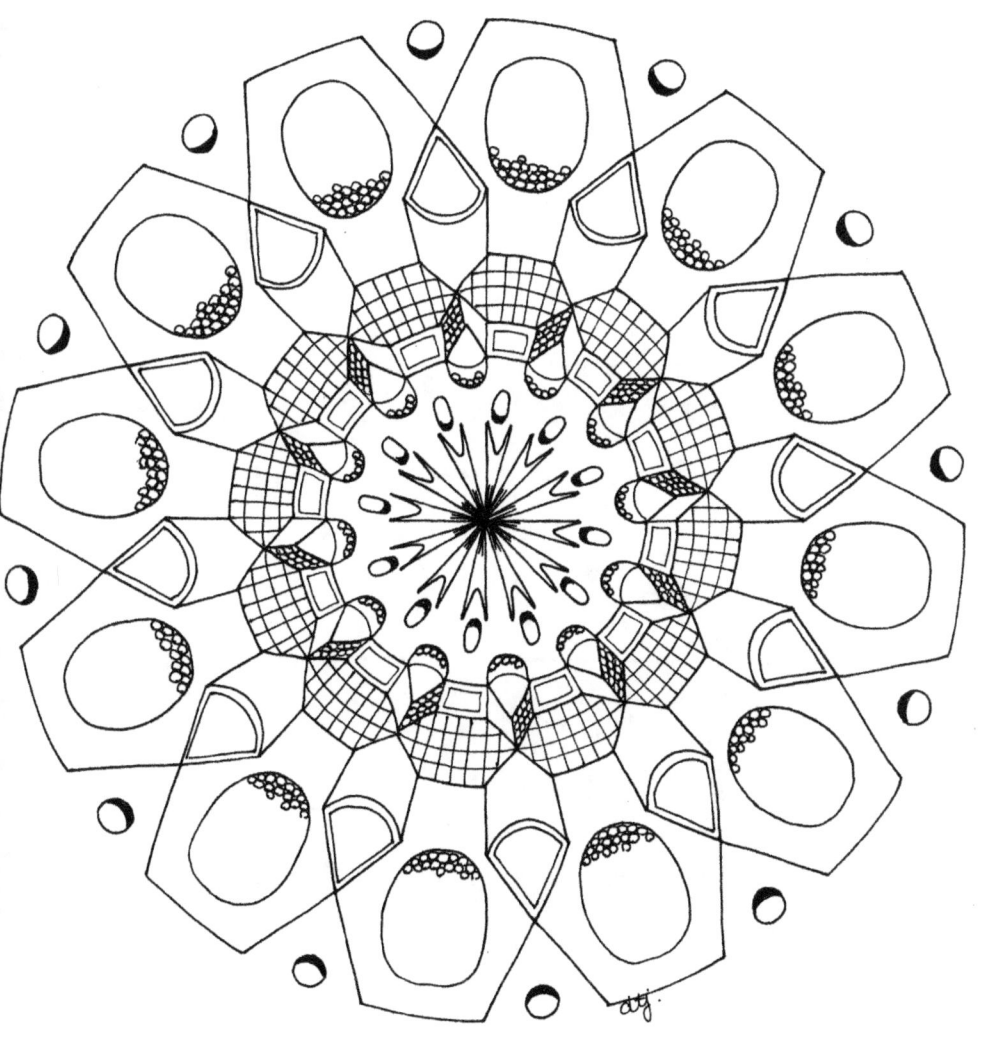

55

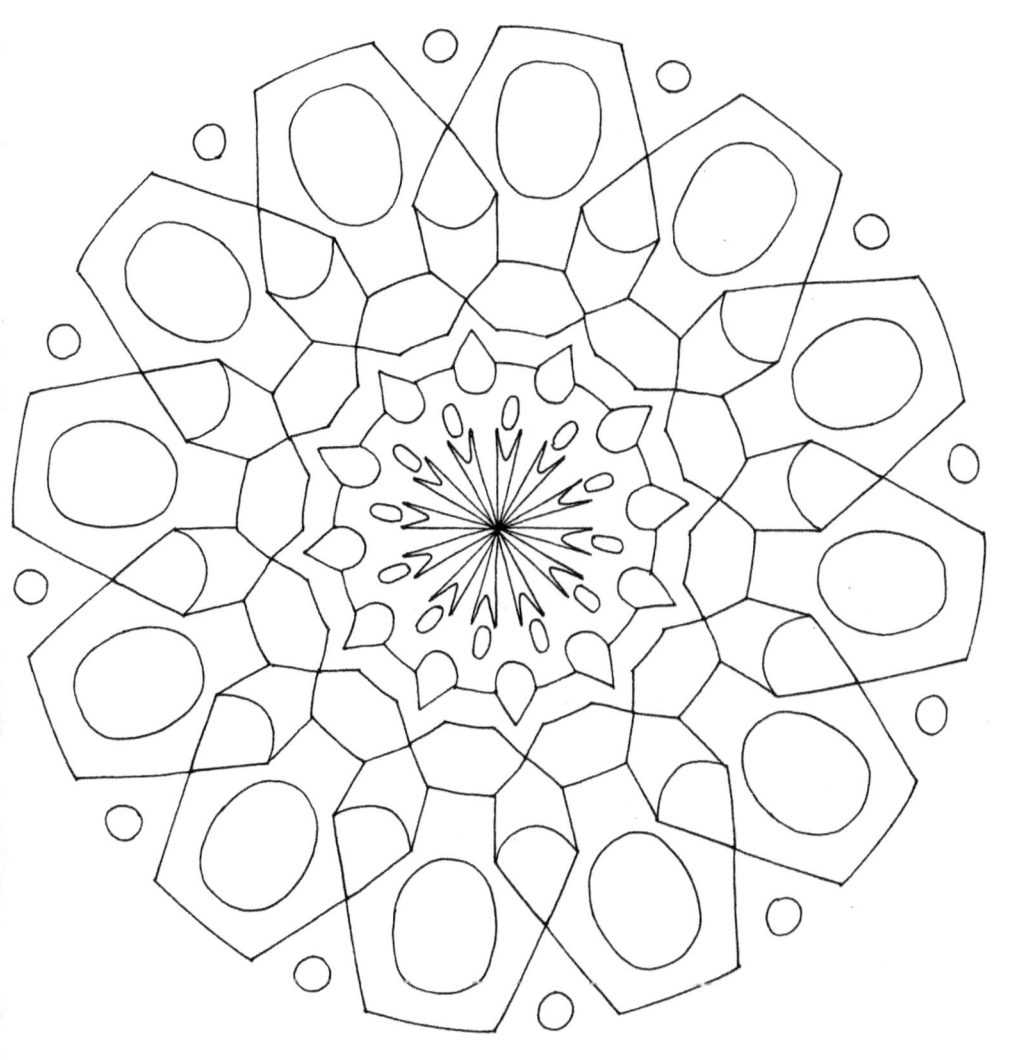

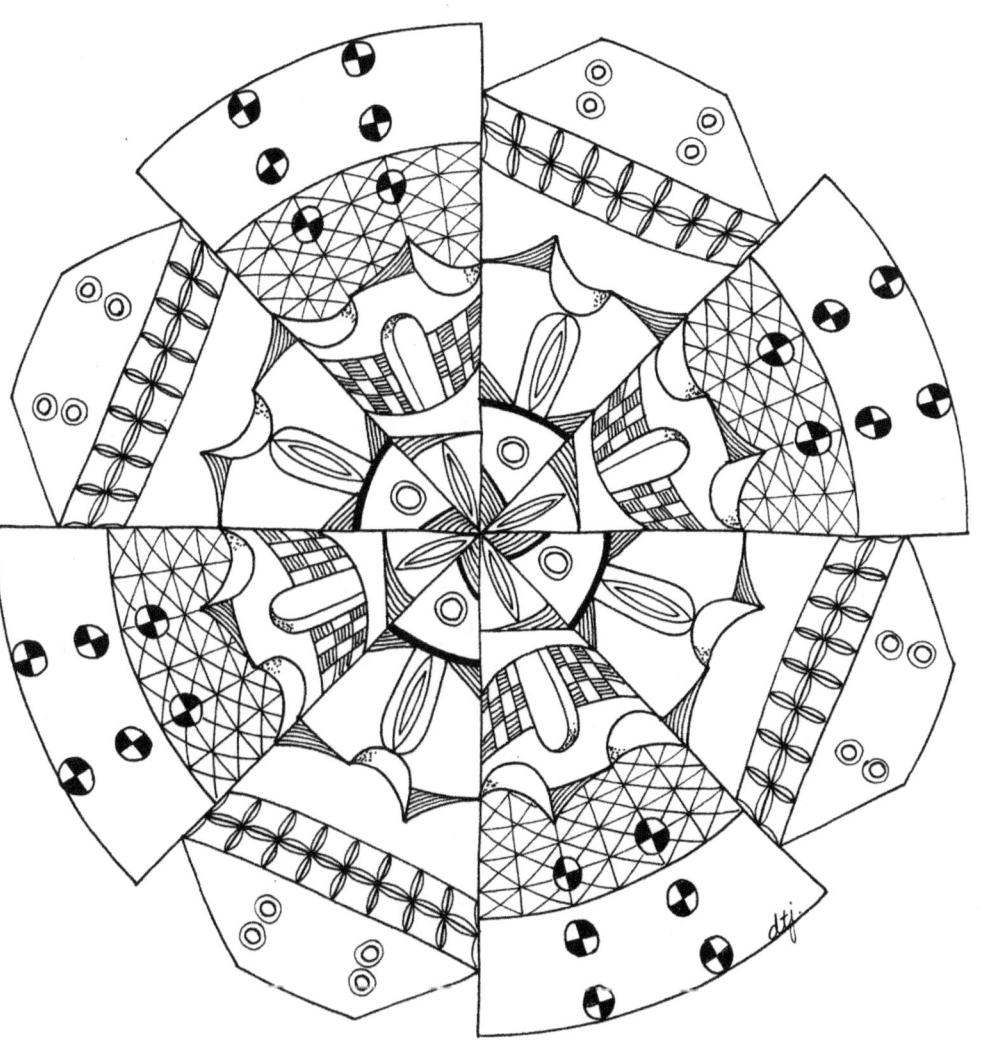

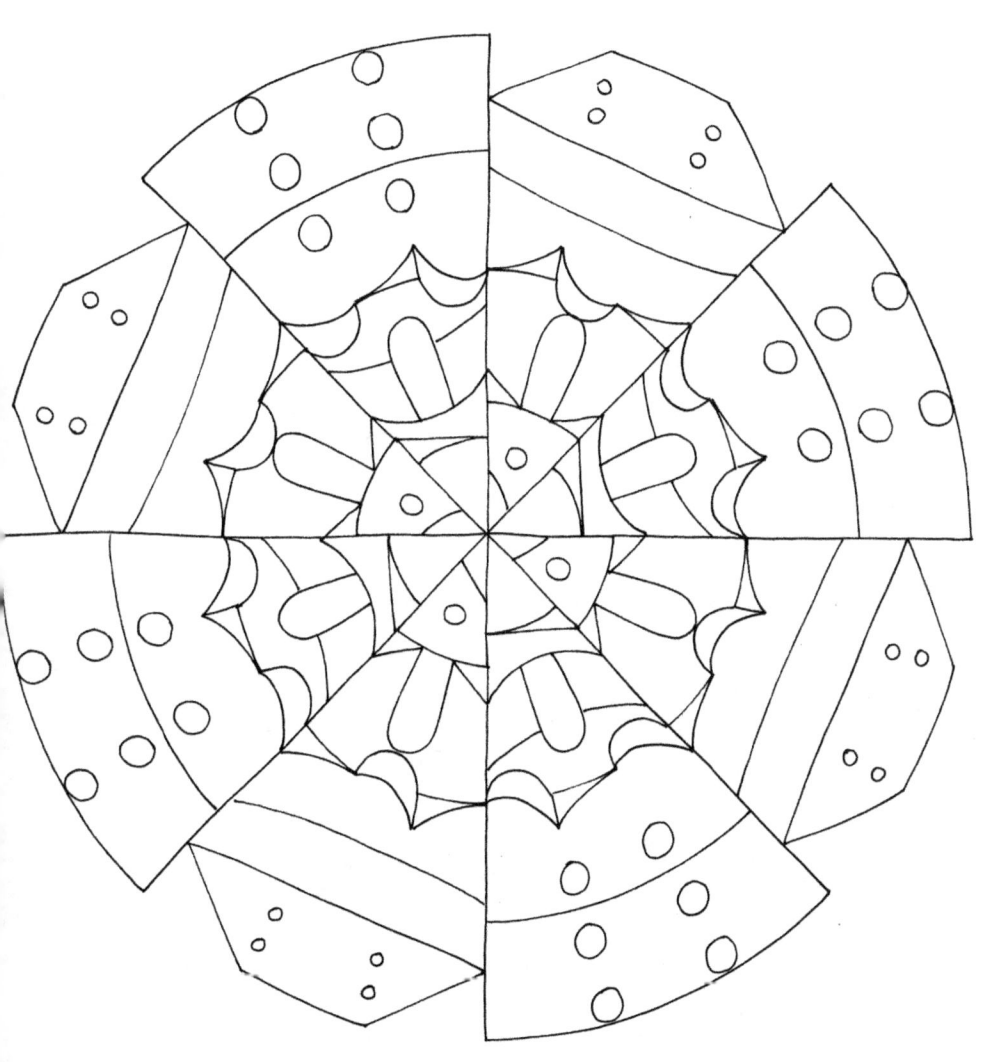

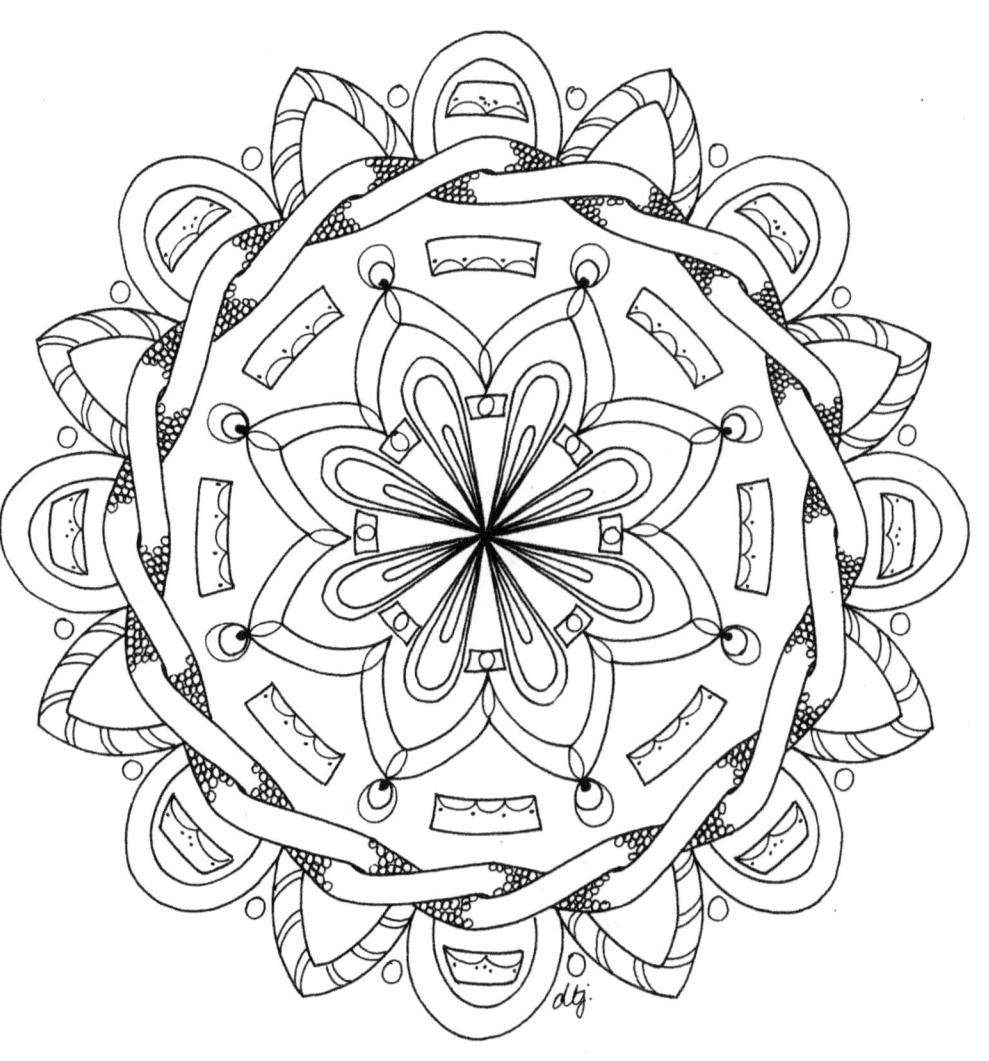

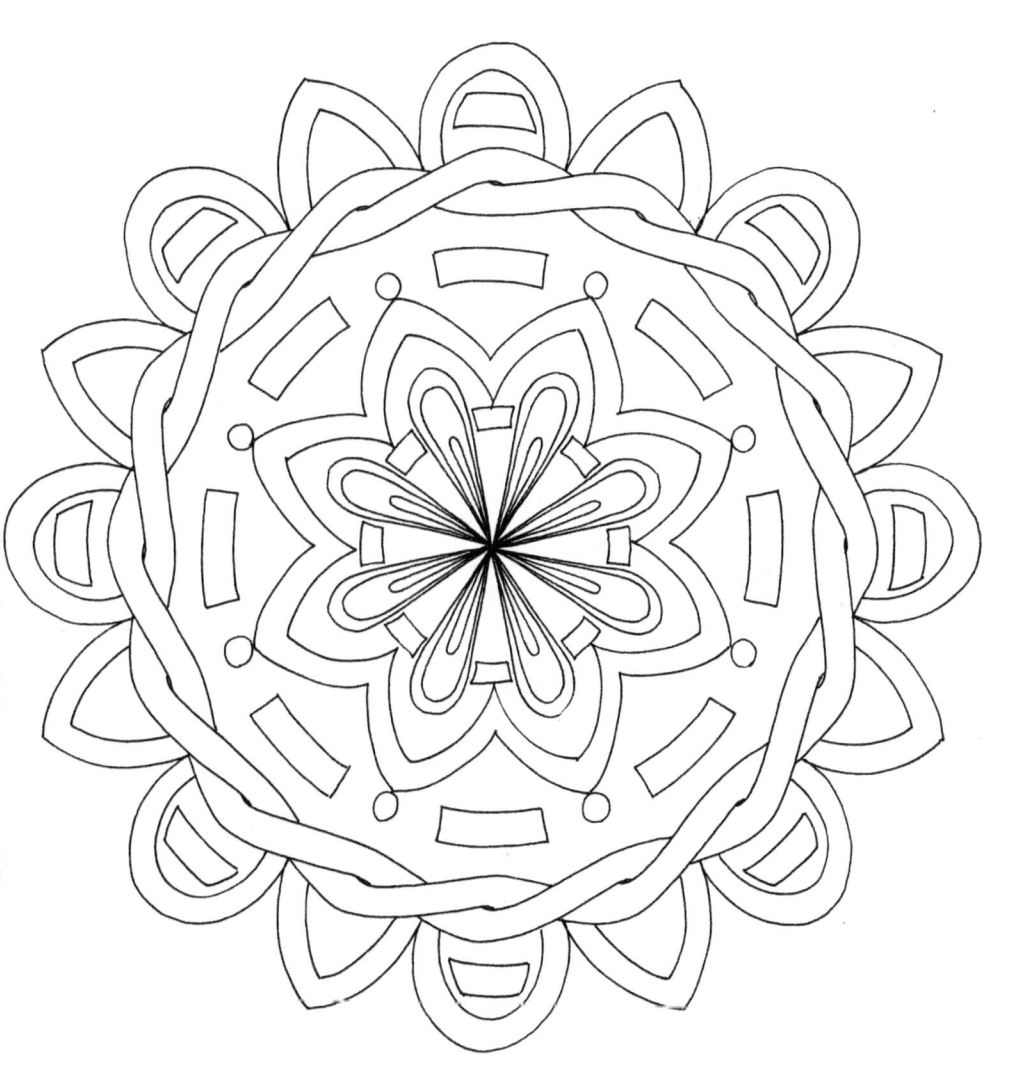

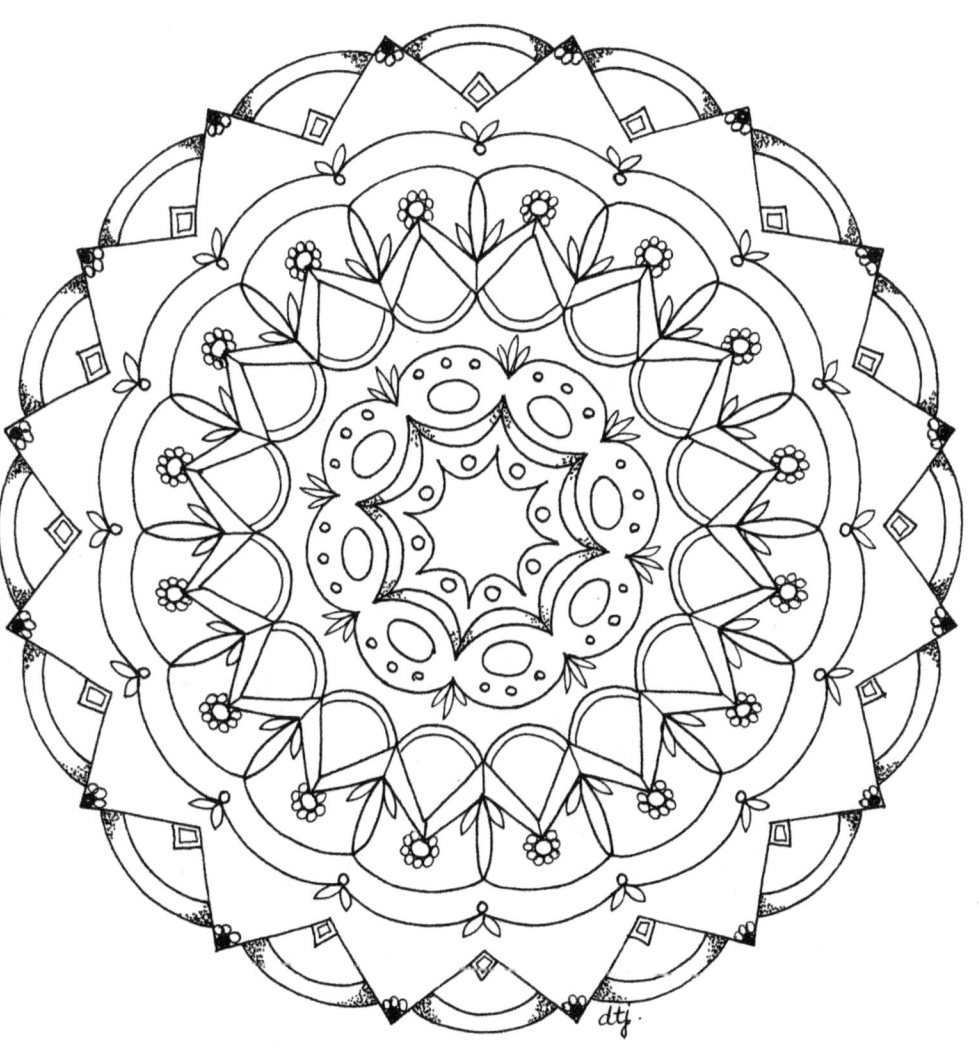

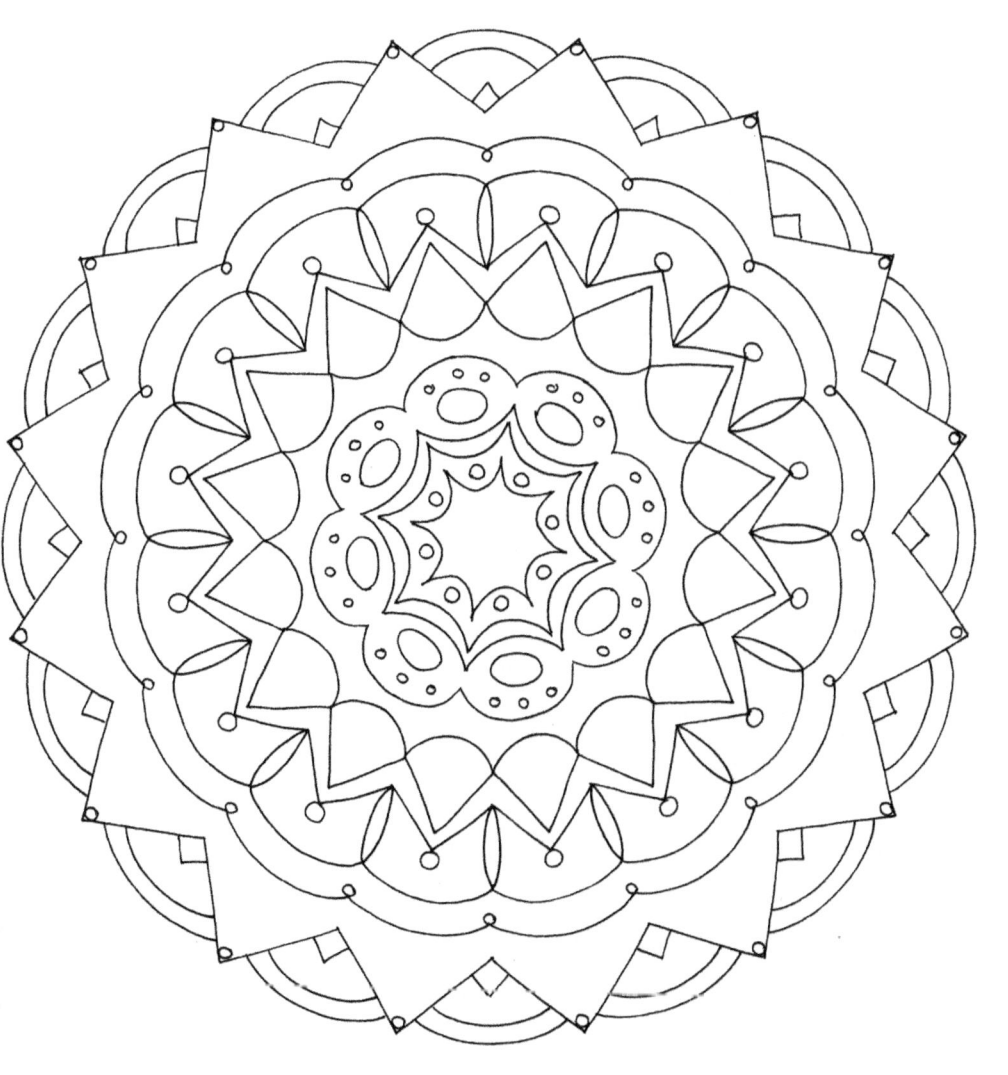

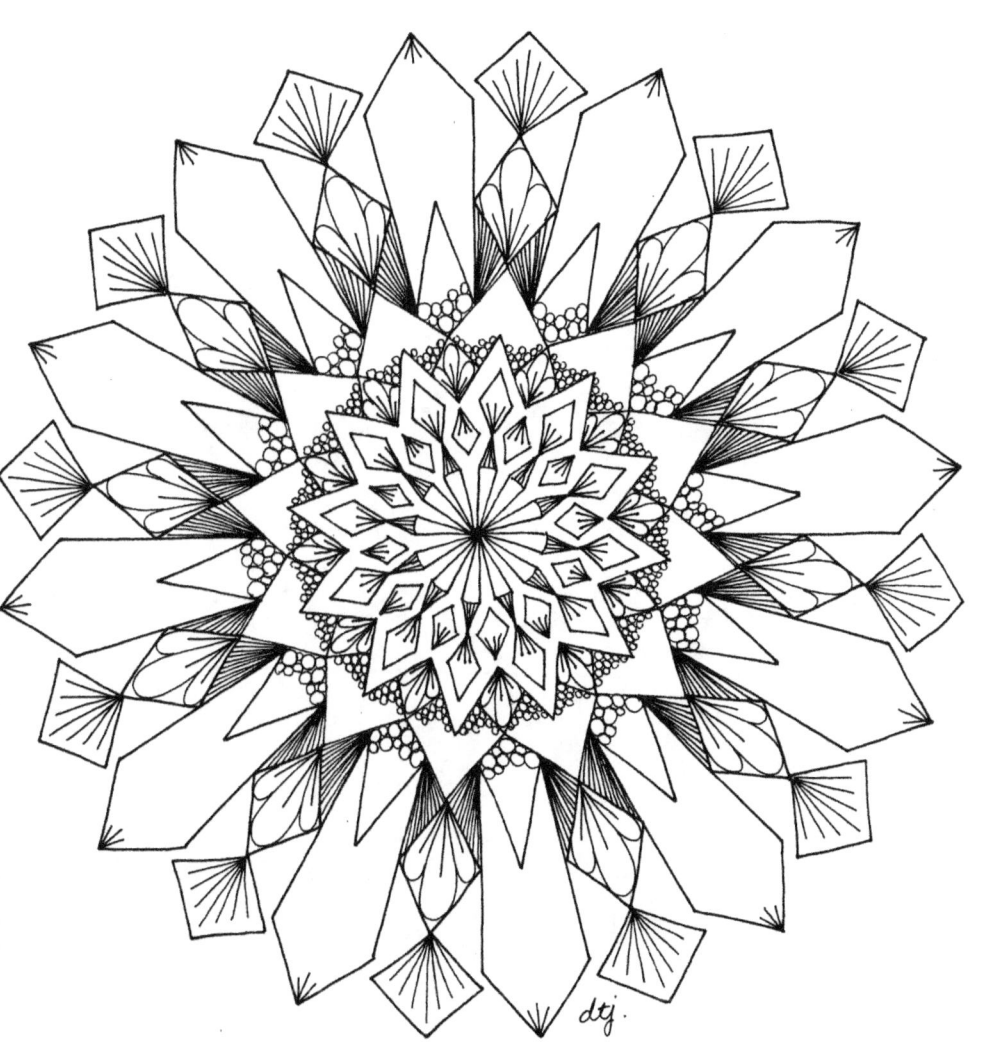

dtj.

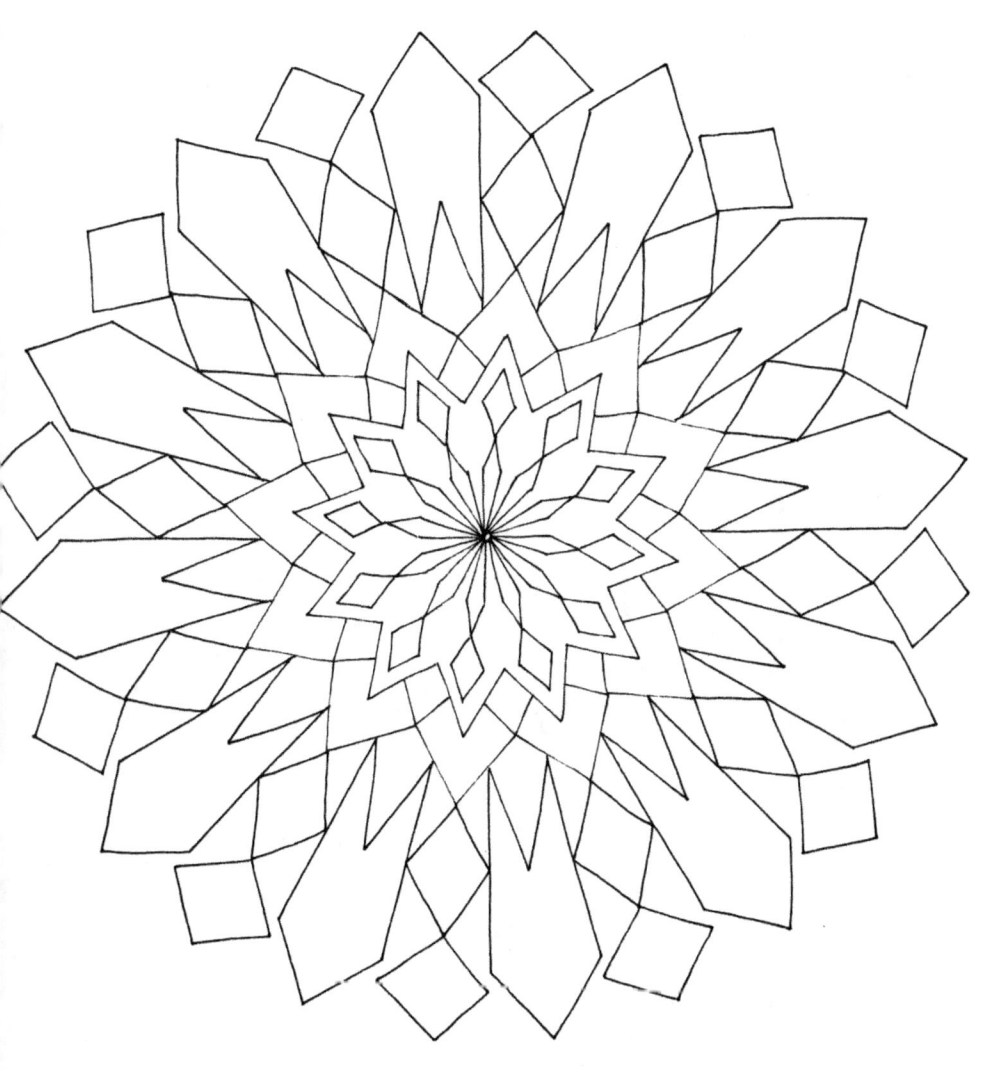

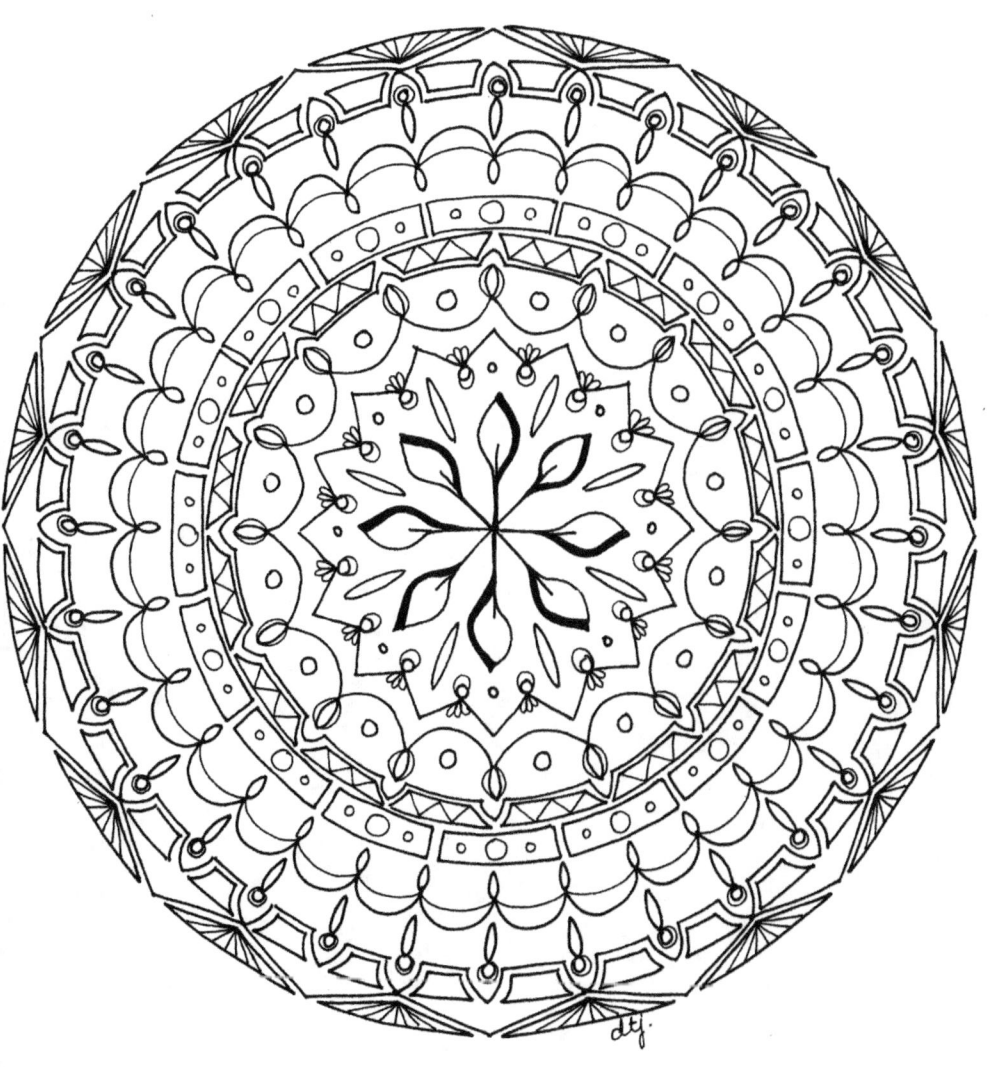

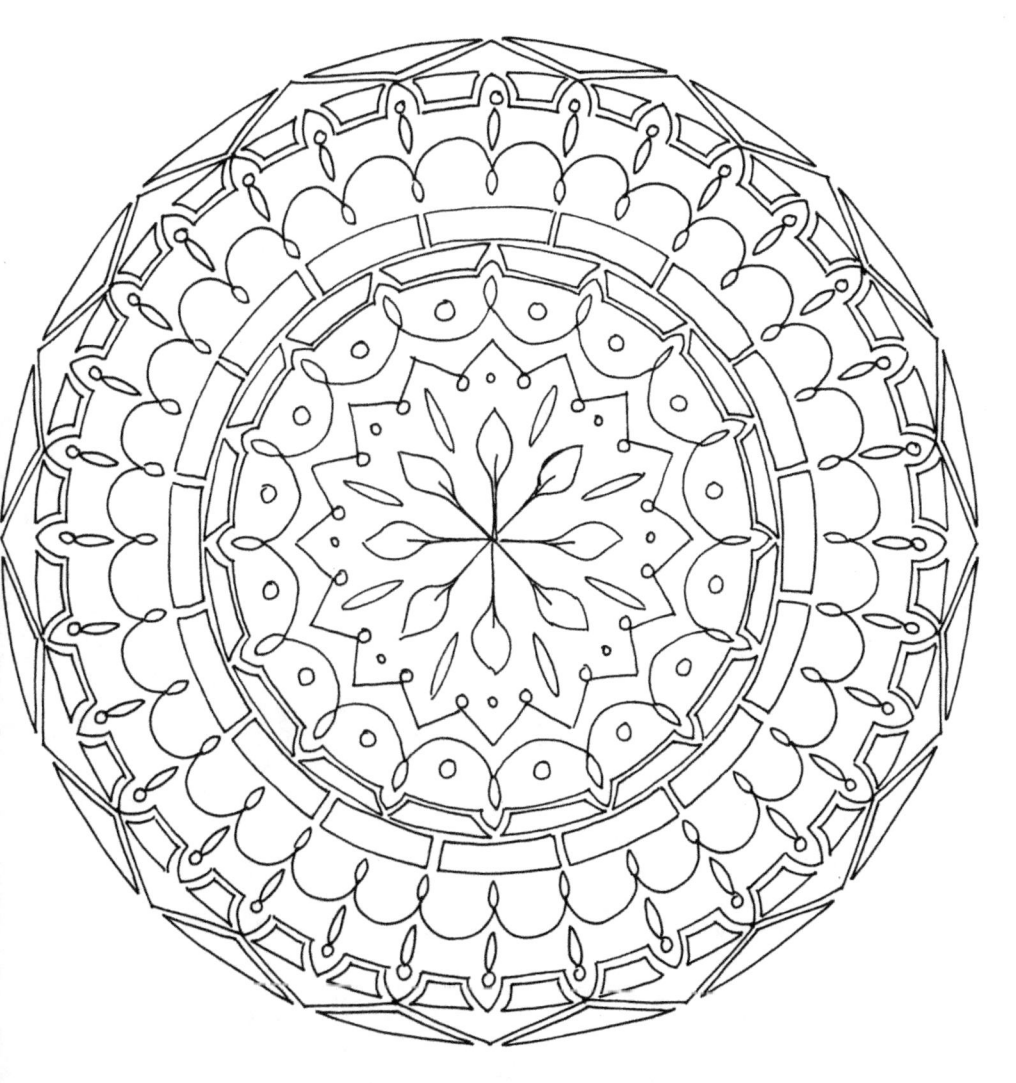

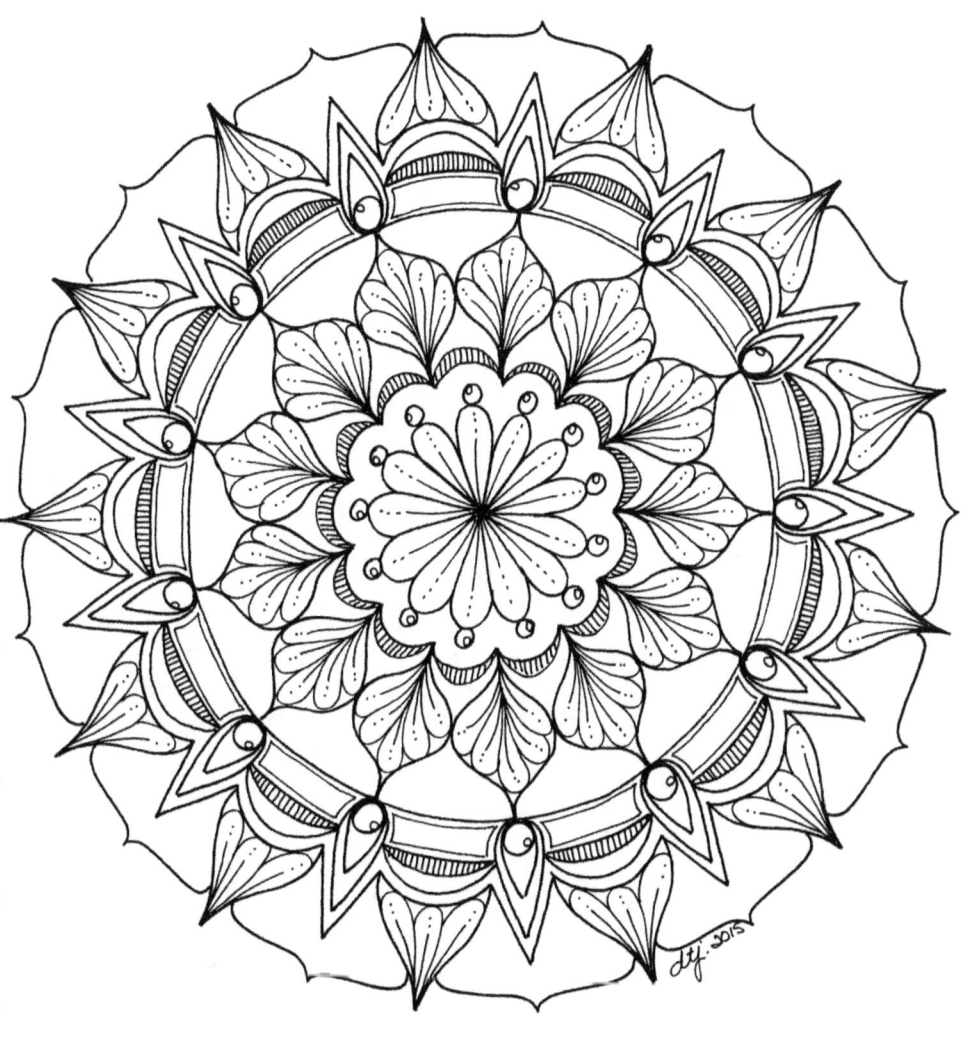

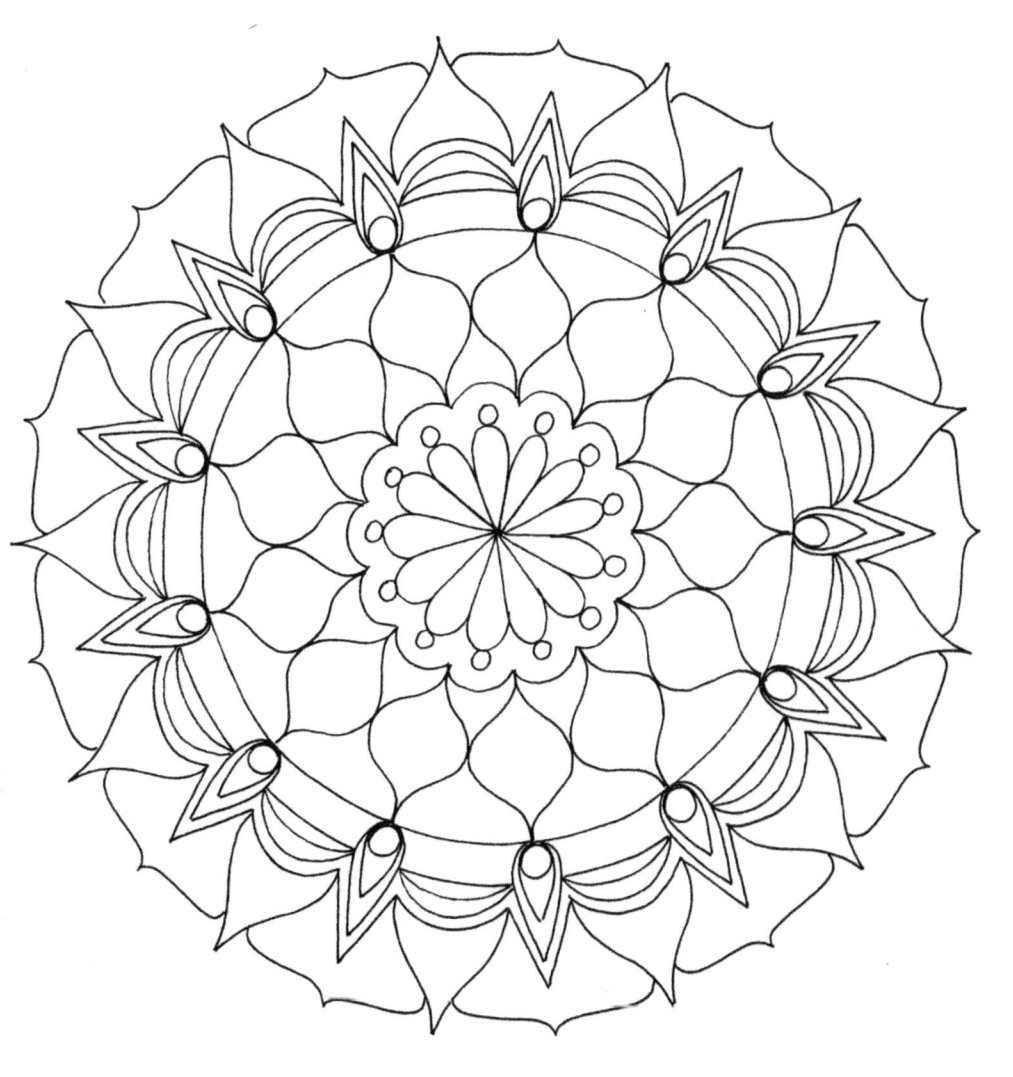

The following pages have some examples of doodle patterns that you can use for your designs. I have also included some other templates that you can print onto cardstock so that you may design your own Mandalas.

Thank you for purchasing this coloring book and I hope you look forward to the coming coloring/doodle books in the series.

Sincerely,

Darla

Here are 72 doodles that you can use to fill in areas of your own
drawings. Patterns are all around us... duplicate the things and

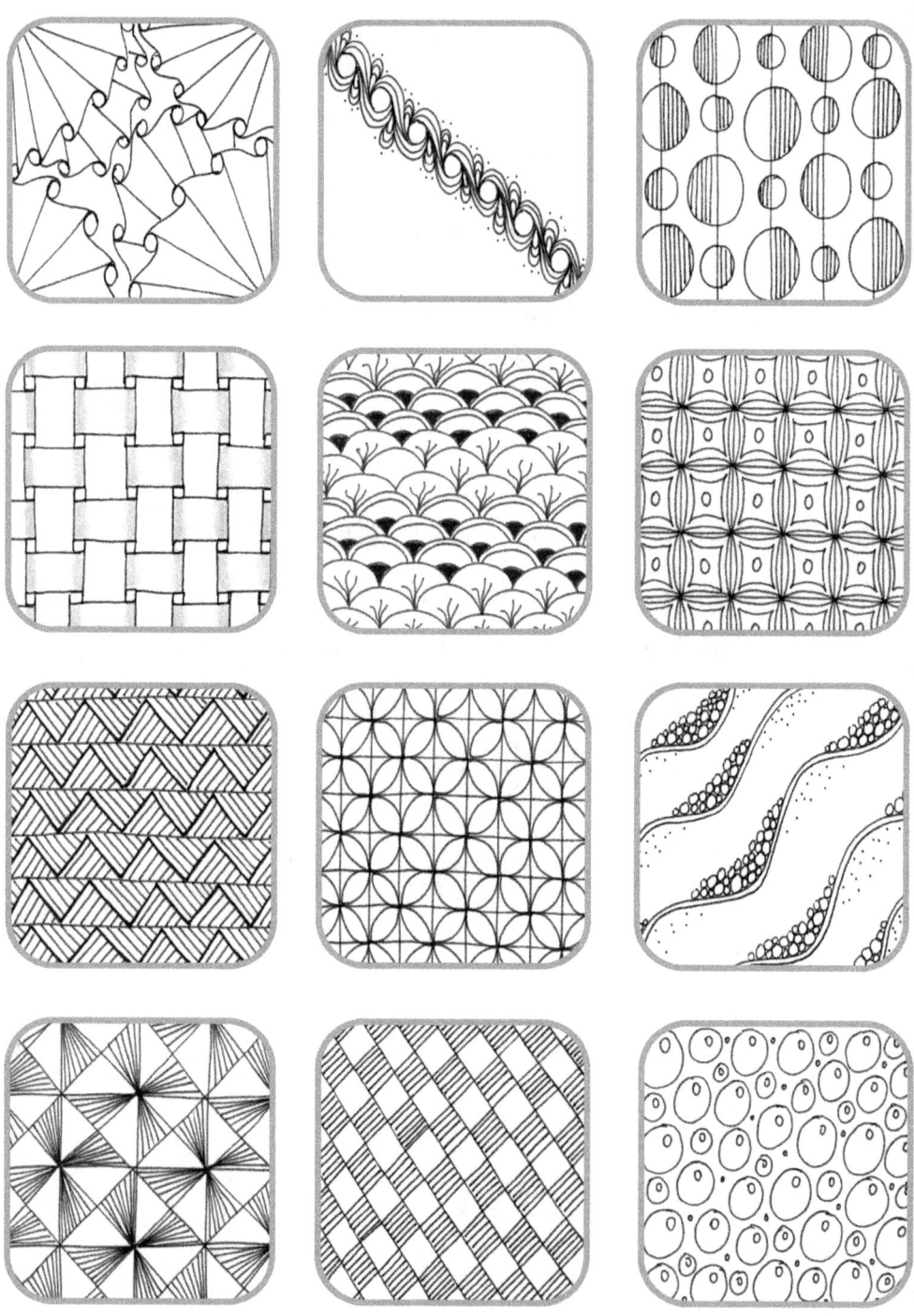

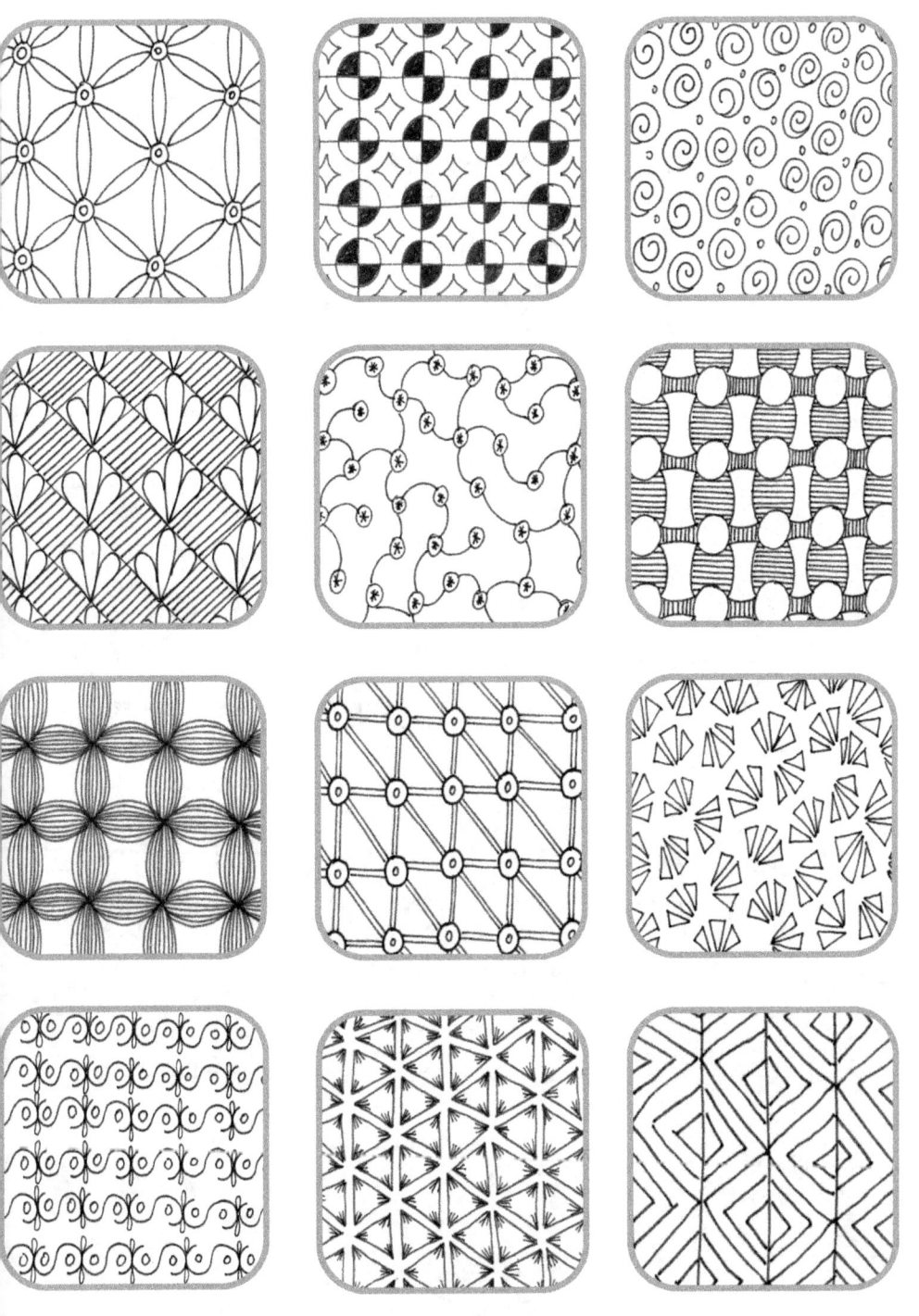

... use your imagination!

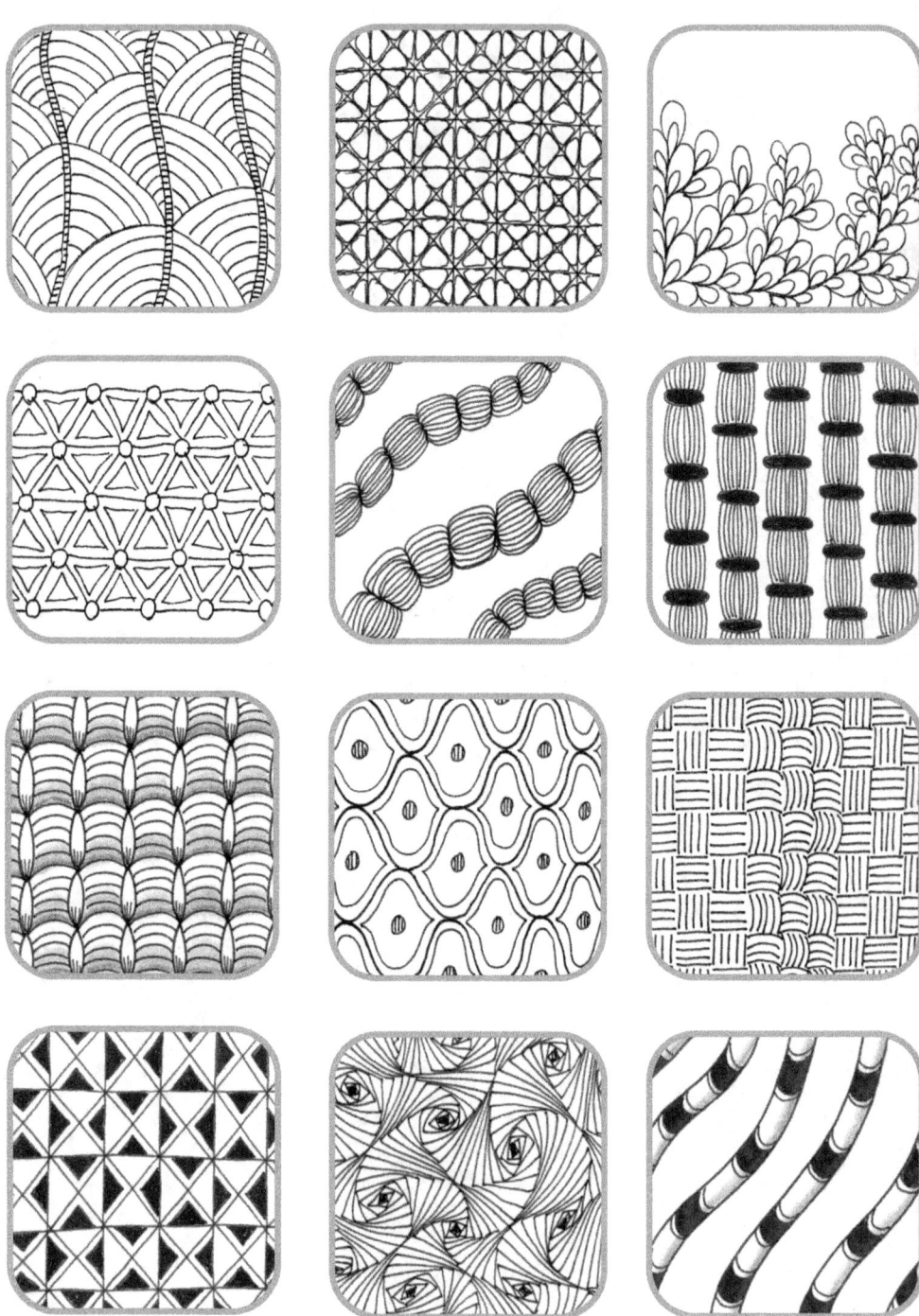

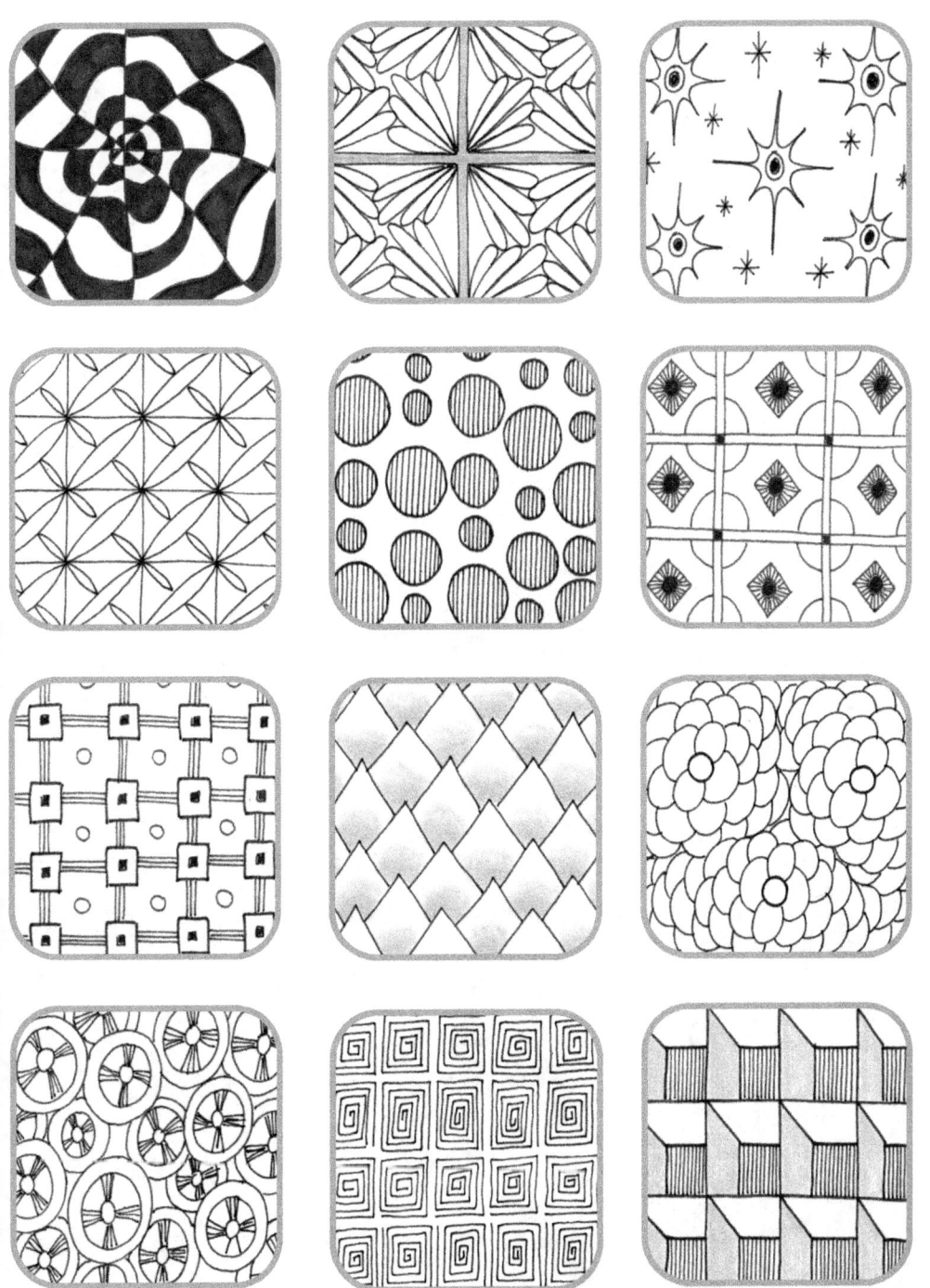

...use shading to add dimension to the doodles.

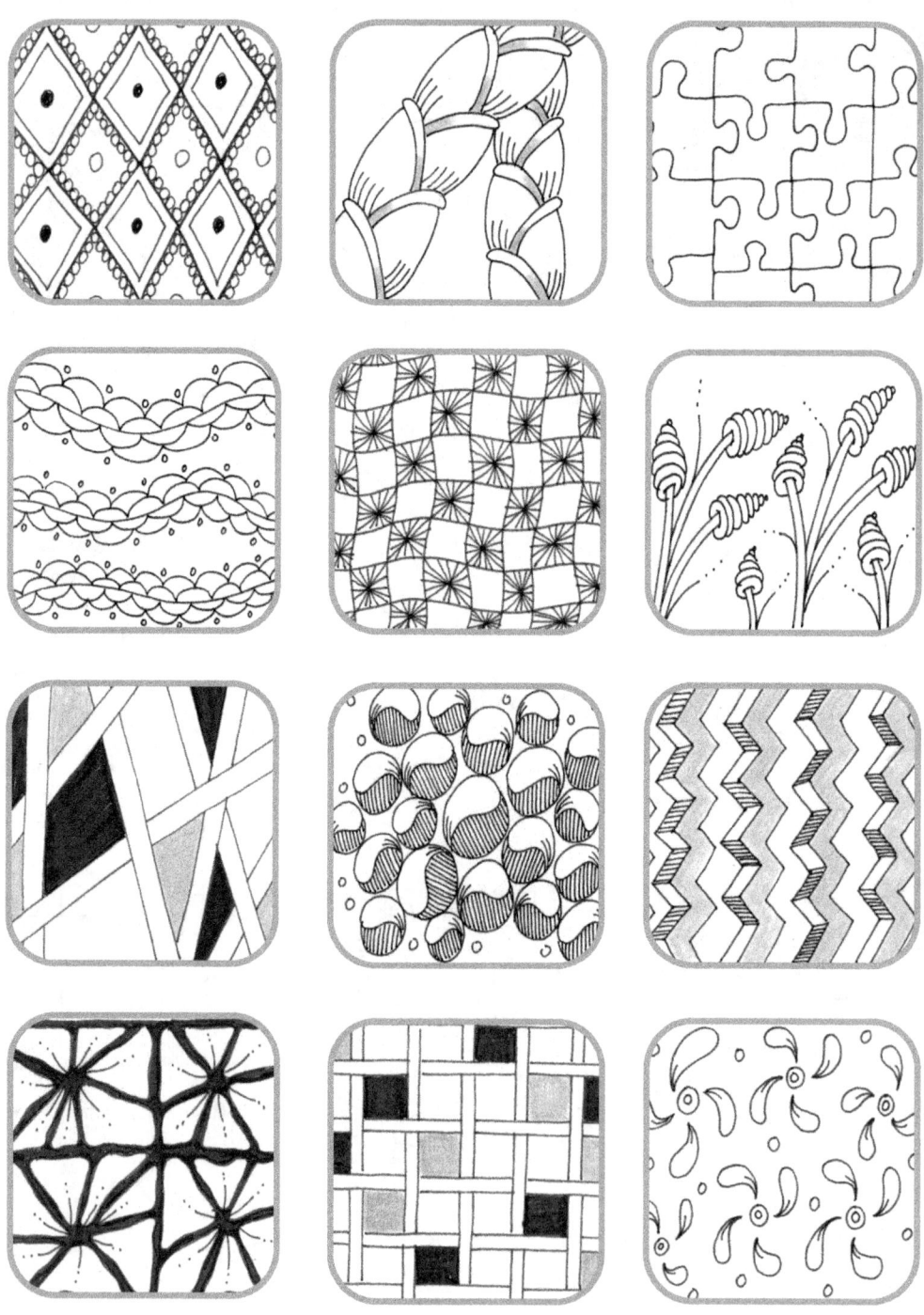

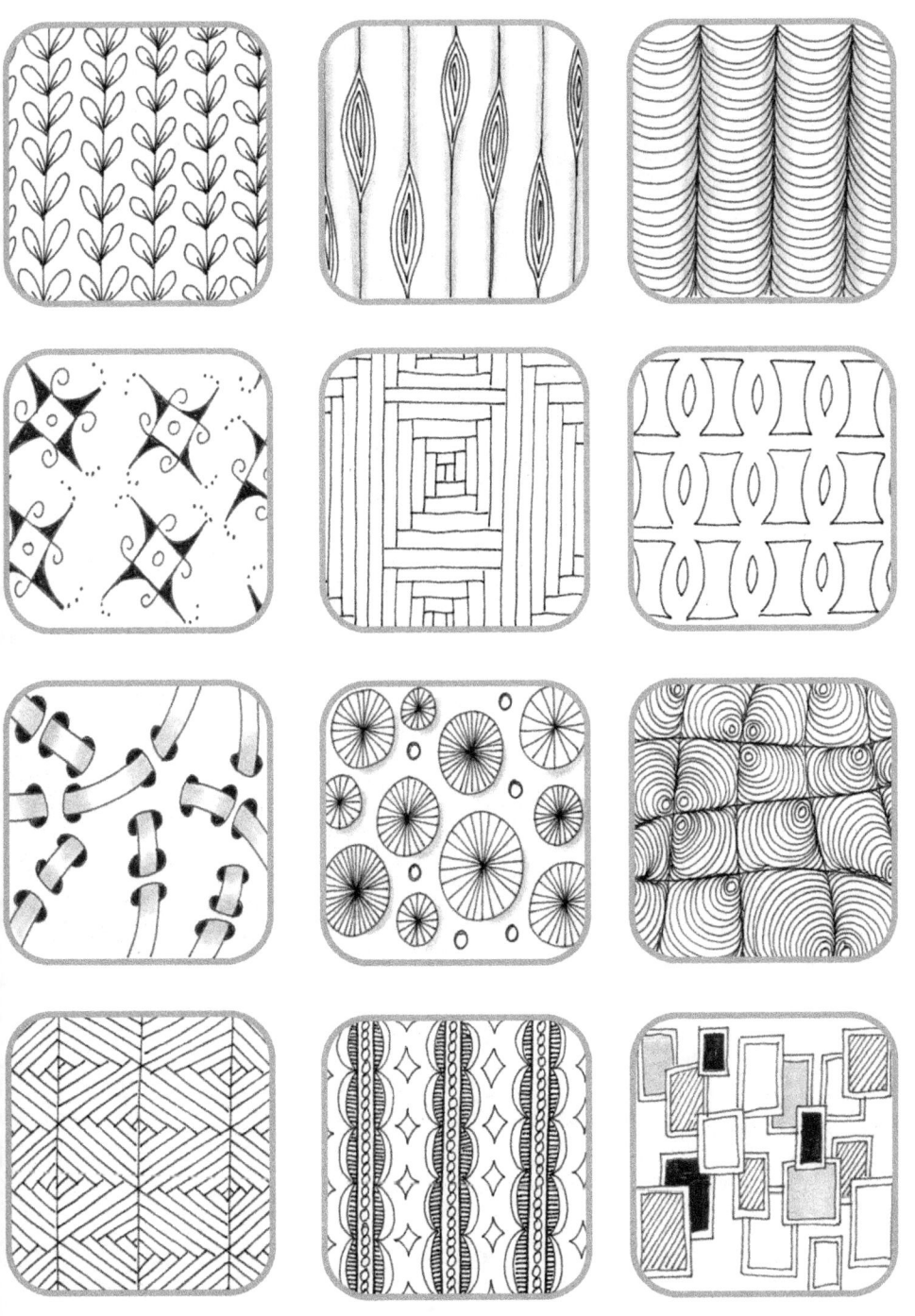

Most importantly, have Fun!!!!

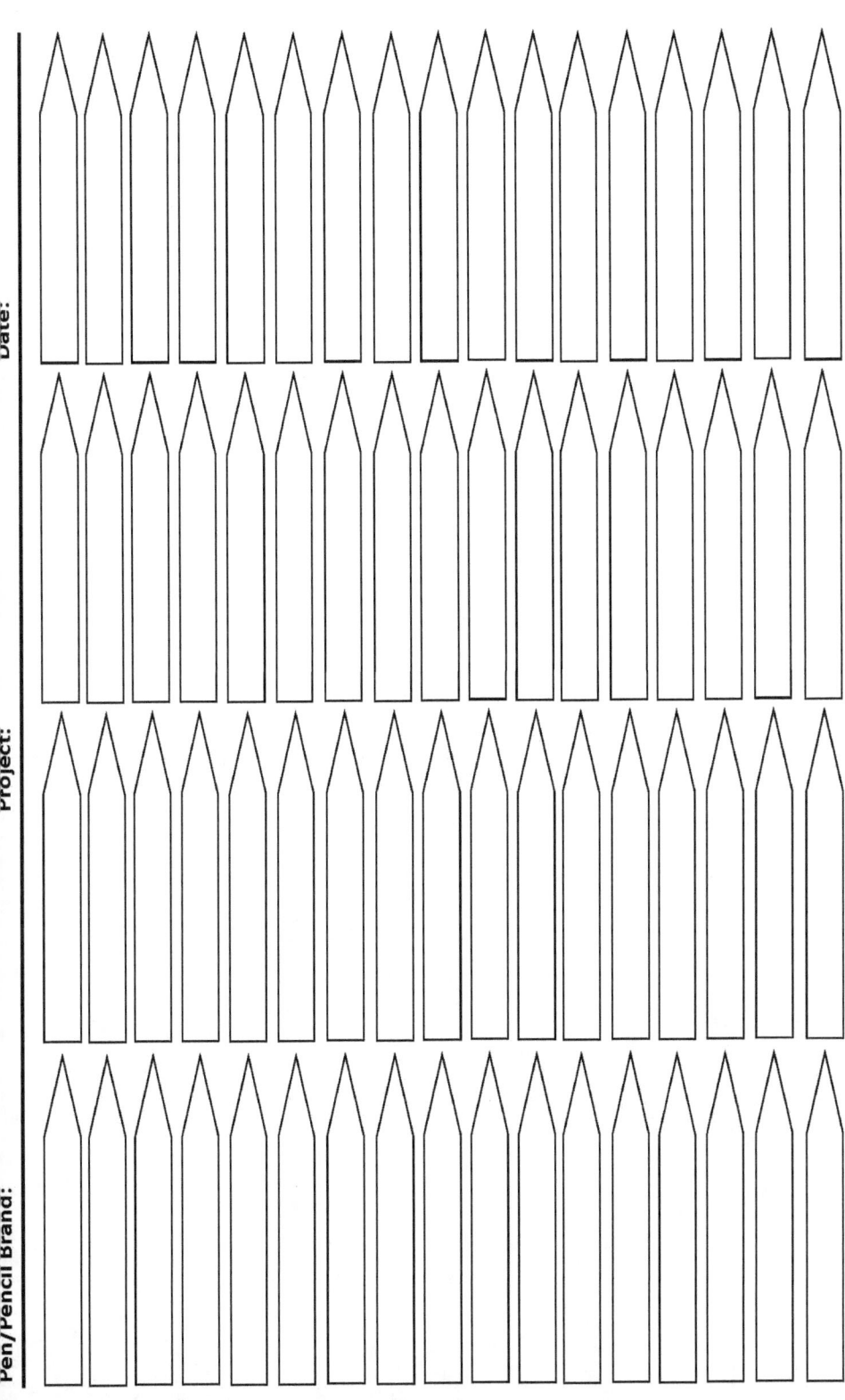

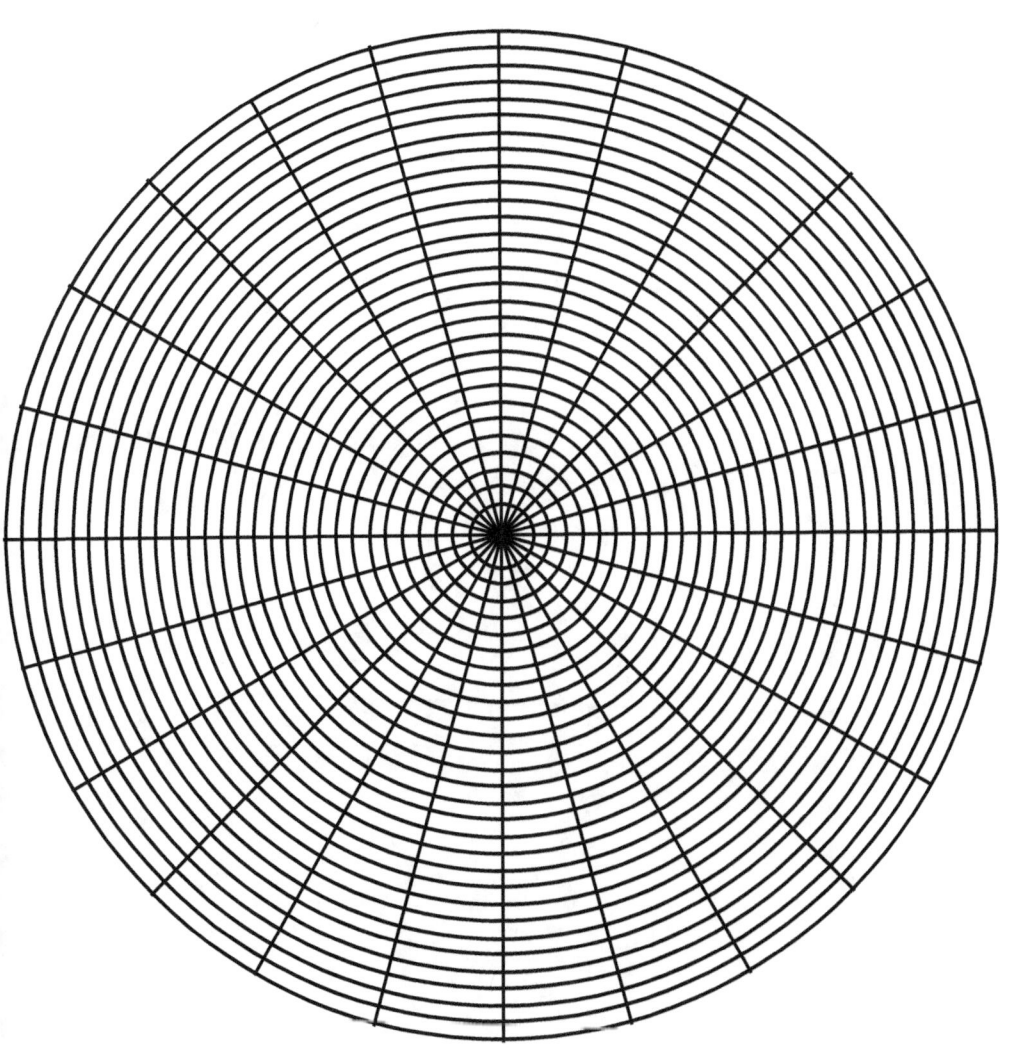

24 Section Reproducible Template for Mandalas

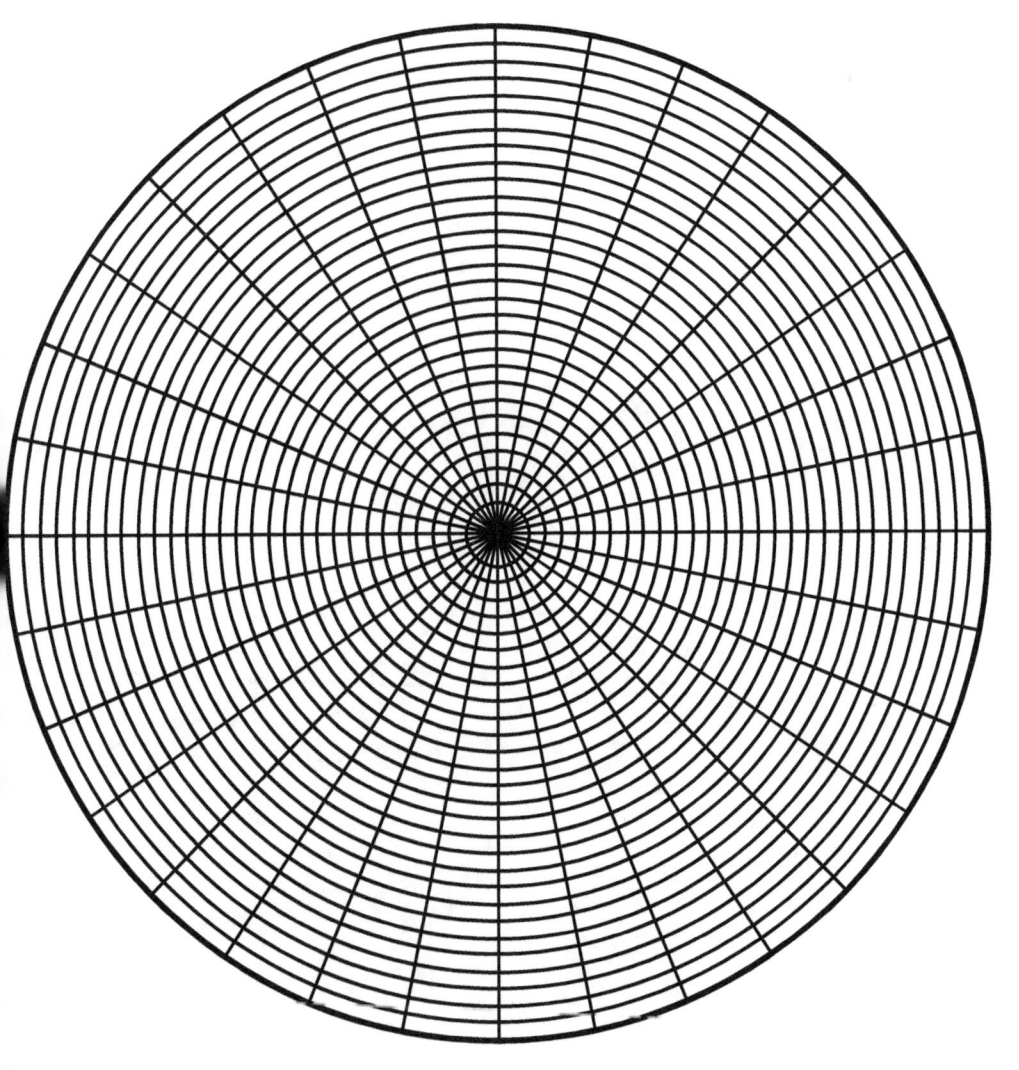

32 Section Reproducible Template for Mandalas